A Man Made of Stories

A Man Made of Stories © 2025 George Franklin

Cover art: 17th century Swedish allegorical painting housed at Skokloster Castle. The Latin translates as "Know thyself."

Author photo: Ximena Gómez

ISBN: 978-1-962405-28-7
Library of Congress Control Number: 2025939778

Sheila-Na-Gig Editions
Russell, KY
Hayley Mitchell Haugen, Editor
www.sheilanagigblog.com

ALL RIGHTS RESERVED
Printed in the United States of America

8/9/2025

A Man Made of Stories

*For Edwin —
I hope you enjoy this book!
With gratitude for your friendship,
George*

Poems

George Franklin

Sheila-Na-Gig Editions

Acknowledgments

Many thanks to the editors and staff of the following journals in which these poems have appeared:

Anti-Heroin Chic: "Against Elegy," "Among Magnolias"
Black Coffee Review: "3 A.M." "At Your Apartment"
Cider Press Review: "The Other Day"
Cultural Daily: "Adam Zagajewski Enters Into Heaven," "Rabelais," "The Body Becomes More Beautiful as It Ages,"
Gramercy Review: "Chinese Food and Polish Poets"
Gyroscope: "The Sulphur Match"
Hare's Paw Literary Journal: "Cambridge" "When Ximena Is Sad"
Hole In The Head Review: "A Poem About the Mind," "Seven Mile Bridge"
MacQueen's Quinterly: "Elsie and Alfred," "In a Florida Prison," "Ode to Stalin," "Sleeping Dogs,"
Matter: a (somewhat) monthly journal of political poetry and commentary: "A Doppelgänger," "Andalusia," "Reading the Classics," "The Memoirist," "The Protagonist"
Meat for Tea: The Valley Review: "Who's to Say"
Misfit Magazine: "Night Train to St. Louis," "The Work of Grieving"
New Ohio Review: "Obituaries"
Nimrod: "Not All That Far From Lincoln Center"
One Art: "Barcelona," "Dog Years," "There Was a Pine Tree"
Panoply: A Literary Zine: "Absence," "An Early Flight"
Pirene's Fountain: "A Question," "How Far Away the World Seems," "In the Afternoon at Las Dueñas," "What's No Longer Here"
Rattle: "It's Yom Kippur, and I'm Not Fasting"
Saw Palm: Florida Literature and Art: "In Florida We Don't Have Mountains," "Without an Umbrella"
Sheila-Na-Gig Online: "A Man Made of Stories," "A Normal Life," "A Persistent Roar," "Avenida Juárez," "Balconies," "Blue Ink," "Conjugations," "How to Be a Tourist in Barcelona," "It Never Rained," "Picking Favorites," "Reading Your Poem," "Such Hunger," "The Flood," "The Hazelnut Child," "The Unfinished Golem," "What the Street Wants," "Without a Soul"
Solstice: "In Heaven"
South Florida Poetry Journal: "A Bench in Venice," "A Question for Borges," "El Café del Sonámbulo," "Jules Supervielle's Beret"

Taiwan & Masticadores: "What Gamblers Know"
The Banyan Review: "Guilty Pleasures," "Hollywood 1975"
The Ekphrastic Review: "At the Museo Nacional," "*The Presentation at the Temple*," "What Brueghel Might Have Painted But Did Not"
The Lake: "A Poem About Loss," "I Was Reading Today," "She Puts Down Her Book"
The Marrow: "*Sobremesa*"
The Wild Word: "In Bogotá," "Watching a Hurricane Pass to the West," "What We Know, What We Can't Know"
Thimble: "Wisława Szymborska and the Wounded Angel"

Special thanks to *WB Yeats Society of New York* and Alan Feldman for choosing "Picking Favorites" as the first-place winner of the 2023 Yeats Poetry Prize.

Thanks also to *The Ekphrastic Review* for having nominated "At the Museo Nacional" for a 2023 Pushcart Prize, to *South Florida Poetry Journal* for having nominated "A Question for Borges" for a 2024 Pushcart Prize, and to American Public Media and Major Jackson for having featured "Picking Favorites" on *The Slowdown*.

Contents

I. Footsteps and Conversation

Picking Favorites	13
What the Street Wants	14
Blue Ink	15
In a Florida Prison	17
A Poem About Loss	18
Ode to Stalin	19
Absence	20
The Protagonist	21
The Memoirist	22
An Early Flight	24
Adam Zagajewski Enters Into Heaven	26
I Was Reading Today	27
Avenida Juárez	28
What Brueghel Might Have Painted But Did Not	29
The Flood	30
The Presentation at the Temple	31
In the Afternoon at Las Dueñas	32
Barcelona	34
"When Ximena is sad…."	36
The Body Becomes More Beautiful as It Ages	37
Chinese Food and Polish Poets	38

II. Soon, the Equilibrium Wobbled

What's No Longer Here	43
The Sulphur Match	45
My Grandfather's Chinese Vases	46
There Was a Pine Tree	47
What It Was Like to Grow Up During the Cold War	48
Elsie and Alfred	49
It's Yom Kippur, and I'm Not Fasting	50
3 A.M.	52
Night Train to St. Louis	54
Obituaries	55
Hollywood 1975	56
Reading The Classics	57

Cambridge	58
The Work of Grieving	59
How One Thing Might Lead to Another	60
Among Magnolias	61
Written on Boxing Day	62
Commuting	64
Sleeping Dogs	65
A Persistent Roar	66
Fingermarks	67
Against Elegy	68
In Florida We Don't Have Mountains	70
Sunday Morning	71
A Normal Life	72
Hawaii, 1968	74
Seven Mile Bridge	75
Dog Years	76
Song of a Prospective Exile	77
Not All That Far From Lincoln Center	79
A Question for Borges	80

III. To Be Alive in Someone Else's Skin

A Man Made of Stories	83
The House in Louisiana	85
Even the Gods Die	86
Without a Soul	88
In Heaven	89
The Unfinished Golem	90
Wisława Szymborska and the Wounded Angel	91
A Doppelgänger	92
A Bench in Venice	93
The Hazelnut Child	94
Guilty Pleasures	95
At the End of a Previous Century	96
Jules Supervielle's Beret	97
One Sky Is Not Another	98
On Revenge	99
Life at the Prado	100
A Poem About the Mind	101
Marsyas	102

Who's to Say	103
El Café del Sonámbulo	104
In Bogotá	105
Reading Your Poem	106
"So innocent the gods"	107

IV. The Lives of Our Desire

What Gamblers Know	111
How to Be a Tourist in Barcelona	112
She Puts Down Her Book	114
It Never Rained	115
Rabelais	116
Without an Umbrella	117
Conjugations	118
Watching a Hurricane Pass to the West	119
Balconies	120
"The Other Day"	122
Andalusia	123
A Question	124
How Far Away the World Seems	125
Drinking Chai on a Mild Afternoon in January	126
Asleep	128
What We Know, What We Can't Know	129
At the Museo Nacional	130
Miami, End of Winter	132
Such Hunger	133
Happiness in the Tropics	134
Unlike Romeo and Juliet	135
At Your Apartment	136
Ximena Refuses	137
Sobremesa	138

*Para Ximena.
Traes dulzura a mi vida.*

I. Footsteps and Conversation

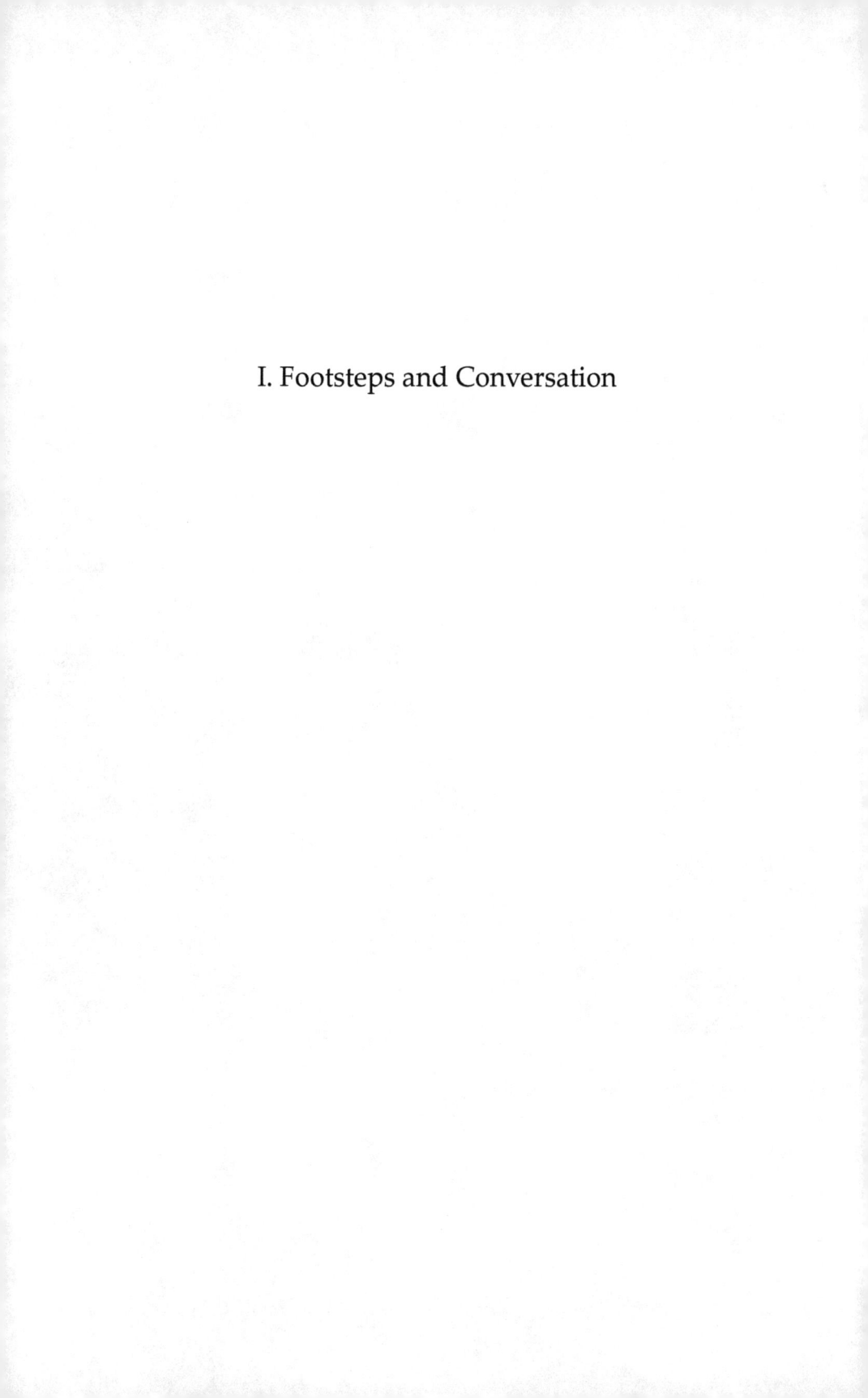

Picking Favorites

We're not supposed to pick favorites.
Whether it's a favorite child, favorite pet (now deceased),
Or favorite time when you went to bed early
And the radio played all the right music—you're
Not supposed to think this way. How will
All the other nights seem if you do? They won't have
Disappeared. You'll still remember them, the holding,
Touching, her lips, yours. You're supposed to say that all
Those nights are equally great, that each child is special,
That your dog the vet sedated with the first shot, then
Killed with the other, was loved no more or less than
The dog after or before, that each house or apartment
Where you've lived has been the dream home you
Always wanted. Get it straight, you're supposed to lie,
To everyone else, to yourself too. Even if you say
You treat each child the same, there are moments
You're closer to one or the other. Sometimes, of course,
You wonder if you haven't failed them all, in different ways—
Times you shouldn't have gotten angry so easily, how
You should have said "Great!"—with conviction—when one
Chose a class in Iranian film over Shakespeare or another
Gave up his scholarship. In Chronicles, David gets into
Trouble for counting the people. It makes sense.
There are things you really don't want to know, like
How many days you've been alive or how many
You've got left. Picking favorites is probably
Like that too. Unlucky. There was the morning in April
When you first walked around Venice by yourself or the night
You and Ximena sat by Biscayne Bay, looking
At the lights from the causeway, the occasional boat
Passing on the water. Don't start counting times like that.
Don't try to remember them either. That way,
They'll stay somewhere inside you, unchanged. You
Can't help it though. You remember how the sidewalks
Dipped in Roma Norte where driveways met the street,
How you had coffee and talked about Lorca. Don't think
Like that. In a little over a month, you'll go back to Mexico,
Order tacos again at El Califa, and Ximena will make fun
Of your dreadful Spanish, and you'll laugh too. That night
Will be perfect, just like all the others.

What the Street Wants

The street that stops just beyond the railroad tracks
Wants to lift its shoulders, stretch to the Gulf of Mexico,
Maybe all the way to Veracruz. It wants to steady itself
Above the waves, arcing like a spark between two wires.

The street that's laid out east to west in suburban boredom
Will not be held by streetlights and signs driven into the ground.
It envies the clouds passing over ranch-style houses, strip malls,
Truck stops, and casinos, clouds that when they're weighted

Down with gray water slide between office buildings,
The plate-glass windows of penthouse apartments going blind
With fog and condensation, their lights invisible. The street
Begins here at a bay that smells of dead fish and algae,

That washes up ducks and jet skis, fumes of marine gas
And feral cats. The street ignores the airport and the planes that
Think only of destinations, time, and profit. The street inhales
The desires of sidewalks and lawns, geometric prisons

Surrounding geometric lives. It exhales tides and full moons,
Horizon lines that are not borders.

Blue Ink

At the prison graduation, the poets stand up
And pour their sadness onto paper plates. The guests
Will take home blue ink and fluorescent light,
Night sweat from narrow bunkbeds, human sounds
Everyone is supposed to pretend they don't hear,
Coughing, crying sounds, the bunk on the right shaking,
Then a sigh and quiet, then the guard counting,
Noisy fans moving but not cooling the air.
For two hours, the guests and the men talk,
Tell each other stories—men from Texas,
Upstate New York, or Colombia; guests from
The same places or somewhere else, sitting on
Folding chairs, the prison band playing jazz standards.
At the first graduations, the bands played rock and blues
Loud enough to make the vending machines vibrate.
It was hard to talk. Now, it's easier. Some of the men
Sit without saying anything, afraid of the guests but not
Showing it, just waiting for the poets, for ink,
For Hialeah twenty years ago or a music festival
On Miami Beach, for triple-deckers in Boston
Or night-fears in Brooklyn or Haiti, grow houses
In Kendall, fathers who floated like river gods
In a noxious ether, violent to one end or another.
It's all ink, on notepad or on skin, stretching
Over knuckles or following the lines on a sheet
Of torn paper, blue ink that stains the guests' fingers.
Last week, a man tried to commit suicide three times.
The first time, mental health sent him back; the second,
He dived off a balcony but didn't die, so he tried again.
They stopped him and called security.
The men speak into microphones, sometimes
Rhyming, sometimes words without ornament,
Words that have been searched, told to crouch and
Cough—and the guests, who may never have
Been patted down before they arrived here,
Hear what the men read, read what the men
Have written. Outside, there is a tree filled with
Starlings and crows, grackles and even sparrows,

So loud the guests can't hear each other when they
Walk by. Sometimes, the crows fly over the wire
To steal scraps from a garbage can. No one bothers
To chase them away. At another prison,
I remember buzzards perched along a dumpster.
There is no metaphor here. The starlings are just noisy
And afraid; the buzzards were patient but hungry. When
The guests arrive, this is what they see. Neither birds
Nor the guests are made of paper, but the words of the men
Are blue ink and fluorescent light. The guests take them home.

In a Florida Prison

He's taped the painting up above his bunk:
Simberg's *Wounded Angel*, bandaged, sitting
On a stretcher carried by two boys, kids
From the street, maybe hired to carry it.
In the background, the lake, a sky in early spring,
Snowdrops blooming sparse and pale. The angel
Holds a handful and carries them loosely.
Did one of the boys give them to her? Maybe.
He can't make up his mind. One boy, in black,
Is a miniature adult. He does what he's told.
The other wears a jacket that doesn't fit and
Carries an angry squint. He's seen men look
Like that before. It's usually just before they
Start a fight or tell a CO to fuck himself.
That look means stay away. The angel's wing
Has blood on it, probably broken, not going
Anywhere. The hem of the white robe trails
In the dirt. From his bunk, he stares at the painting,
Sky, water, the boys' hands gripping the poles
Of the stretcher. He remembers an owl
That used to perch on the fence at night,
Claws wrapped tight around coils of wire,
Wings stretched wide before it flew.

A Poem About Loss

Years later, I'm still writing the same
Poems, Eden that isn't Eden, the past that
Was never Eden. Dying of old age
Isn't simple. At least, it wasn't for my
Parents or their parents. No reason
To think it will be for me either. Last week,
I was in a nursing home on a law case.
There was a woman 100 years old,
Deaf, and mostly blind, but she wasn't
Ready to die. A Buddhist monk told me
Once that we get used to suffering, and
After a while, we think pain is normal.
But it's hard to get used to the world.
I remember my oldest son teething
At 3 months, crying without pause as
I walked him much of the night.
I don't know if walking him helped
His pain. Maybe it just made me think
I was doing something to make him
Feel better. It was only a few steps
On an old wooden floor. I turned
At the radiator and walked back toward
The door to my bedroom, then back
To the radiator. Sometimes,
We'd walk the room in a circle, and
Sometimes, I'd recite whatever poems
I knew by heart. The woman in the
Nursing home had cancers covering
Her face. Within a month or two,
The worst of my son's teething was
Over. Sometimes, I'm still back in
That room, walking him.

Ode to Stalin

No, this is not exactly what it purports to be.
The Stalin of my title is not that 20th century ruler of the USSR.
Rather, he is a young man, alive now, in Mexico City who
Came up to me after a reading and asked me
To sign his book. I confess, his name surprised me,
And I asked him to repeat it. He did, and I dutifully
Dedicated the book to him. Afterwards, I imagined that
His father had been a party member and named him
Stalin in a moment of pure hope that his newborn
Son would change the world, that he would foment a fierce
Unbending revolution, end the suffering of the poor and
Punish the rich, the drivers of American and European cars,
The people to whom tacos are "street food." But fathers
Often get it wrong. An infant's face can't tell you much
About the future. I would bet money this Stalin is a poet himself,
A reader of lyrics, a romantic moved by the way words
Can touch each other, innocently, the way a woman
And a man walking on the wide concrete outside
The Palacio de Minería might look up at the rooftops
And then back down toward the pigeons, and down
Farther still to the carved stones and Aztec sacrifices resting
Undiscovered, so many meters beneath the street.
What novels are you reading, Stalin? What films do you like?
And what possessed you to buy my *poemario* and ask me
To sign it? Perhaps you turned down the wrong hallway
At the bookfair and heard my friend Omar Villasana
Announce the reading was about to start, or you saw those
Huge windows in the salon, wide open, their curtains
Flapping like white sails or birds' wings. Maybe you just
Needed a place to sit. The corridors and the long
Staircases of the Palacio are exhausting. And the book?
Did you read it? I'm embarrassed that I didn't ask you more
About yourself and write more on that title page. By now,
You're likely working or studying at a university,
And the book I signed—with its poems for Ximena and the one
About my father's orchids—is forgotten, wedged tightly on
Your shelf, between Lenin's critique of imperialism
And Gramsci's Prison Notebooks.

Absence

I want to give my students that Linda Gregg poem about absence,
But then, I think that they already know more about absence
Than I do or even Linda Gregg did. Every week, before
The guards let me inside, my shoes, jacket, belt, and papers
Rumble through the X-ray machine, and I'm patted down
To make sure I'm not bringing in contraband, which includes
A lot of things you might not expect, like stamps or a letter.
I've followed this routine for eight years now. Every week,
I bring in poems, which are their own kind of contraband.
But, I was talking about absence, which is more than grief
For a person you've loved or a place you can't go back to—
The absence they know is a life that never happened,
One lived outside the gates and razor wire. They don't
Talk about it, and I don't ask—but sometimes it stares out
From a poem or a chance remark. Then, like one of the starlings
That land on the trashcans, it flies off over the fence, and I
Exit the clanging gate, climb into my car, and drive away.

The Protagonist

In movies and novels, the protagonist turns the key
In the ignition, leaves entanglements in a lopsided
Rear-view mirror. He doesn't bother to adjust it
Because what's abandoned isn't important. He passes
Prairies and mountains, coyotes crossing the highway at
Night, truck stops full of flannel shirts, caps, and bad coffee.
Stopped somewhere up ahead, Walt Whitman is waiting.
Jack Kerouac eats apple pie and vanilla ice cream on
A stool in a diner. Gary Snyder cooks stew in the desert.
The winter constellations are fireworks against a black sky.
But, it's all wrong. Walt Whitman died in Camden
And Kerouac in Florida, surrounded by conservative
Magazines, beer cans, and bitterness. The road ends
Where it started, a cliché like a sour stomach. The protagonist
Ages badly. Whatever he thought he'd find, it wasn't
Where he thought he'd find it. Arthritis invades his ankles
And his hands. He doesn't draw the same breaths anymore.
Whitman was supposed to be waiting, but he never
Showed up. In New Orleans, in the morning, they're washing
The sidewalks in front of the bars. The strippers have gone
Home to sleep. Trucks collect green bags of garbage on
Bourbon Street. It's Sunday, and the Cathedral is open for
Business. In the park, the statue of Andrew Jackson
Continues to tell the same lie. Bukowski was thrown in
Jail in Texas. At the water's stubborn edge in California,
The protagonist finds an absence he can't talk about.
His thoughts sink in the waves, like sea glass or books
He won't read again. At rush hour, the traffic slows
Without any obvious reason. He wants an ending that's
A real ending, one where everything make sense.
Instead, there's just traffic going nowhere.

The Memoirist

The open road always begins somewhere else,
Not so open. The story begins with the absence
Of story, a recollection of childhood illness,
A room with the shades drawn, fever, adults
Whispering as they shut the door. The hero
Will cross deserts and picture-book mountain ranges,
Ride through the snow on horseback or sip
Small glasses of liqueur with a countess, will
Know just the right moment to lock eyes
And touch. When he returns home, he vows
To be discrete, but memoir abhors discretion,
Revels in climbing over rooftops like Giacomo
The Venetian, to escape and move on. He is
Five years old, and they wake him because
The doctor is here. The black bag yawns,
And a hand withdraws a hypodermic. There
Are pills and blood tests, bored aunts who read to him
From Charles and Mary Lamb, who fall asleep with
Their mouths open, heads dropping as they speak.
The memoirist sits in cafés drinking absinthe with his
Well-known friends. He doesn't like the taste but won't
Admit it. There's a fly in the water pitcher, and the woman
Across the room refuses to notice him no matter how
Loudly he speaks. He tells a story about being robbed
In New York, his attacker running away. It seems
To him that no one is paying attention, or perhaps he's
Told the story before. He can't remember. Taxicabs
Turned off their lights and kept going. Byron swam
The Hellespont despite his club foot and had the bad
Luck to die from wounds in battle. The road
Isn't as open as it appears. Cellini made art to earn
The pope's forgiveness. The memoirist changes hotels.
That one was drafty. You could hear the water closet
Drip from down the hall. What forgiveness exists
For crimes that never happened? His memories
Are lies, mechanical inventions, automatons that
Dance or play cards. There was a gazebo, a wet cheek,
A kiss that flattered only the teller, not the tale,

The lips reluctant and closed. The automaton
Requires a wind-up, then begins to dance, shifting
Its metallic weight from one foot to the other.

An Early Flight

Poems arrive at the least convenient times—

Actually, it's the memories that arrive: tungsten reflected from black water, the stone dock on the canal, the salt chill coming off the lagoon, knowledge that in a few hours you will be encased in metal and traveling over everything that matters, including the clouds.
Or, what matters will be left behind here, a lost suitcase filled with clothes and books, with all the ridiculous fantasies of how you could be living elsewhere, how you could wake to the noise of wheelbarrows in the street, Adriatic light through the gaps in the curtains, how the morning would yawn across the Giudecca, the vaporetti moving back and forth like toys.
The plane will give you plenty of time to sleep, so that last night you look out the window, the campo dark with darker shadows— you imagine cats stalking sly old rodents who chew into the plastic bags put out for collection, the rich scent of garbage— then footsteps and conversation, a couple walking back to wherever they live, walking over stone bridges and through the narrow passageways. You imagine them relaxed with each other, touching the way people touch who know each other well. A moment later, you no longer hear them.
You are waiting for the water taxi where a passage between buildings ends at the canal. Delivery boats unload at docks on the other side, oranges and radicchio, televisions and space heaters, almonds and mushrooms. Everything costs more because of how much work it takes to get here.
Each year, the water rises, a little or a lot. Palazzi have lost entranceways to the water. The city does not tell lies. Nothing lasts. You are one of millions of intruders, rubes who pay their money to ride the Ferris wheel, throw darts at balloons. You are tolerated and deplored. Because of you, the rents are unaffordable, the vaporetti too crowded.
You want to think you're different, but you're not. The campaniles cast their shadows and ignore who watches them, who climbs their steps. The clocks periodically require repair, but they gesture nonetheless, with the arms of a cop managing traffic. Time is a commodity. The days you spent here are over. The

churches are filled with paintings, but they shut their doors last night. It's too early now for worshipers or for gawkers like you who drop coins into boxes that turn on the lights.

Admit it. You're afraid to return. You know yourself better now, know your fantasies for what they are. Wherever you stay, you'll be a tourist. You have no business here. You stuffed the things you saw, crumpled, into a carry-on, a postcard of the Bellini triptych at the Frari folded in the middle, the afternoon sun on the tin roof of Il Redentore, boats being repaired in shipyards. It's been too long. Your youngest son is grown. Your marriage ended. And, you're happy now in another city.

That morning, before dawn, when the canal speaks to itself in an unintelligible language of lapping water and wet stone, when the heavy wooden doors of palazzi are bolted shut, and you're still half asleep, when you can't see beyond the electric light by the alley—that morning shows up just when you should be doing a dozen other things, when it's already long past dinnertime on that other continent, the city you used to dream about, where the restaurants have already closed, the opera house has emptied, where no one knows you, and where the only people you could visit are those illustrious dead on their walled island.

What is it that matters now? Why do you remember your son imitating the architecture with his wooden blocks, the waiters in the cafés with those immaculate white jackets, and you walking in the morning to the fish market, buying tuna and squid, then gorgonzola dolce from a shop nearby? How long did you tell yourself this is what matters, a city that existed in your sleep and in images, a city of alleys and docks, of closed doorways and glimpses of gardens?

You were wrong. These images never belonged to you. You borrowed them and had to give them back. The water taxi arrives on time, and you load your bags, sit on a padded bench in the cabin. The driver follows the channel out to the airport.

Adam Zagajewski Enters Into Heaven

If there is a blast of trumpets, it's pitched higher
Than a dog-whistle, too lofty for human ears,
And the angelic chorus hums suspiciously like
Crickets in a Polish field in summer, a low
Buzz that stops at the sound of footsteps
In the dry grass.

                Enter then the poet, improbably
Descending from a railroad carriage, pre-war
Vintage with wool seat covers and woodwork
The color of honey. He opens the door
Of the carriage and, as stated, descends
To the platform constructed from prayers
That didn't require an answer. In heaven,
Everything has its purpose. Of course, there are
Other travelers already moving toward
The great doors of the station, where outside,
Their relatives, lovers, friends who died young
Wait impatiently to welcome them. Some are pranksters
And hand the new arrivals an unexpected gift,
A toilet plunger or a pepper mill. They enjoy
The look of confusion on the bright immigrant faces.
Others hang back, the way Dido did when she
Saw Aeneas. They remember too much.

But for the poet, there is no welcoming committee,
No angels with cornets and drums, no banners
Or tall, black-suited chauffeur holding a sign
With his name misspelled, no car waiting at the curb.
He walks carefully and alone across the plazas
And over the bridges of this new city. He doesn't
Seek to ascend higher than the canals
And walkways that stretch parallel lines
To a painter's infinity. This, he tells himself,
Is enough. Sunlight rests on the terracotta rooftiles,
And a waiter in a starched white shirt pulls back
A chair, inviting him to sit. He can smell coffee,
And watches croissants float in straw baskets
Above the café tables. He makes himself comfortable.
There's no reason to hurry.

I Was Reading Today

I was reading today about an explosion
Eight billion light years away. A black hole
Swallowed a cloud of gas and quietly

Released energy the size of a galaxy.
It made me think about beginnings and
Endings, and how the universe is nothing

Like ourselves. We may not remember
Being born, but we know it happened—
And we've seen plenty of people die.

So, we argue about whether something
Came out of nothing or whether something
Was here first, because we want to think

The stars are just a larger version of
Old men walking around the block,
Knowing that before long, a niece or

Nephew will have to make the phone call
Beginning with "I've got some bad news…."
We want to think our corner of the universe

Is a giant child who one day just appeared
In the garden, where a childless couple
Found him among the daffodils and

Raised the boy until he grew too large
For the cottage doorway and looking
In the window said good-bye.

Avenida Juárez

Saturday night crowds Avenida Juárez
With families, students, kids off work, vendors
Selling tortillas, candy, roasted ears
Of corn. A girl skips rope on a path through
Alameda, the park starred with tungsten,
Shadowed by jacarandas. Accordion players
Cluster the sidewalks, pass the hat for pesos.
The grand Palacio de Bellas Artes looms,
An architectural cocktail shaking out
Art nouveau, deco, classical, stone and glass,
But the steps are good for resting, couples kissing.
Tomorrow morning, the Zócalo will be
Packed with protesters wearing pink t-shirts,
And hats, the metro closed, the streets blocked,
But tonight is for the singers, microphones,
Ballads, and Mexican hip-hop dancers—also
For two poets, a Colombian woman and a
Norteamericano, who are filled with
A great happiness to walk down such a street.

What Brueghel Might Have Painted But Did Not

In the courtyard, men are unloading wagons, and there's
A horse waiting to have his saddle removed, to be
Rubbed down and given oats or autumn hay.
One merchant talks to another, perhaps his partner.
They wear thick wool cloaks, and their gloves are soft leather.
They do not notice the horse or the men in the courtyard.
They're concerned with important things: how to get a load
Of lumber to Antwerp, what it means to have such an early
Snowfall, the Baltic amber someone is offering for sale.
The silversmith at the inn kept talking about it. He'd had
Too much to drink, but still…. On their shoulders,
You can see white specks of snow starting to melt.
The horse paws at the paving stones, untended.

The Flood

After the ark had left its improvised dock—
The waters having risen quickly—the animals
Not selected or boarded in time were abandoned
In treetops and on high hills. They watched
As the great ship drifted south or north or
Maybe west, its outline shrinking in their
Sharp eyes, in the waves. But the animals,
Being animals, said nothing. For sure, they
Knew it was unfair. All the fish would survive,
Even sharks and bottom-feeders. But the parrots
With their red and yellow feathers would
Tire eventually and fall out of the sky,
And the lions and elephants would sink
To the ocean's muddy bottom—sand would
Come later. Spotted deer raced wildly for a while
On the steep slopes, their hooves splashing
Water behind them. Dung beetles bored tunnels
Into whatever earth they could find—not because
They thought it would save them, but only
Because that was their habit. A few hares tried
Desperately to procreate for the same reason.
Why does no one praise the nobility of the creatures
Rejected by Noah? Many had waited in line for days.
Some, the gnats and flies, had spent a lifetime
Buzzing in place, waiting to be admitted. They
Must have known that even the highest mountains
Would be submerged. But the wet slow-moving tigers
Only paced in a circle, growling at nothing,
As ordinary pigeons continued to preen
Their gray iridescent feathers, and a troop of
Brown monkeys with large eyes and delicate fingers
Still picked lice from each other's fur and
Stared at where the ark had been.

The Presentation at the Temple
   —Giovanni Bellini, c. 1460

The room smells of their sweat, perfume, and oils.
Light stirs the dust gathered beneath his easel,

The folds of her robes. Bellini has sketched her
Often, and he can follow the curves of her lips,

Her eyelids, without thinking about it. He
Hasn't yet chosen a model for the child

Or for the high priest, but the priest's robes
Will be a red brocade and the child swaddled

In linen, prepared already for his grave.
For the Madonna, only a light scarf,

No halos or other evidence of divinity.
Her earlobe pierced, but without a ring, she'll hold

The child upright, close, and the priest's hands
Will reach across a parapet. Time stops.

The witnesses will glance side to side,
Cautious as prisoners awaiting execution.

In the Afternoon at Las Dueñas

Pero yo ya no soy yo,
Ni mi casa es ya mi casa.
—Federico Garcia Lorca

Bougainvillea grows purple on the wall,
Purple sunlight reflected on stucco, on the yellow
Clay of walkways between the orange trees.

In the reflecting pool, I see the same white hair
And beard, nose a little sunburned, face
Unprotected, puzzled—a lost dog, it's looking

For its owner, but no one has come to claim it.
The sun sinks lower than the rooftops, darkening
The leaves of the orange trees. The purple

Bougainvillea sinks lower on the wall. Perhaps, I've
Also turned purple in the shade of the orange trees,
In the light of the bougainvillea. Unseen, this face

Moves lightly up the staircase, through the tiled
Hallways. It doesn't glance at the statues. It doesn't
Notice the paintings. The face does not belong

To anyone now. The oranges it tasted were sour,
They shined from the tree limbs, sour orange stars
In the daylight of the bougainvillea, the shade

Of green leaves, darker than black, the white wall
Of the convent that closed long ago, the patter
Of the ticket-seller in the afternoon heat, date palms

Taller than the house and the walls. In the heat of
Bougainvillea shedding light like a dying star,
In the acidic perfume of white blossoms,

In the darkness of leaves and the yellow clay
Of walkways that twist through the garden, I
Raced to catch up with you, your pink blouse

And scarf the color of roses disappearing
Between orange trees and the last sunlight
Of the bougainvillea, between a fountain

And a face that used to be mine.

Barcelona

Down the street, a dog is barking, and pigeons
Coo in reply, a low trill that celebrates the end
Of daylight, mares' tails floating in from
The Mediterranean. Perhaps, in Mallorca,
A different set of pigeons are making the same
Sound, and a different dog is barking to be let inside.
Perhaps, the mares' tails have floated there as well.
The courtyard is quiet this evening. A few voices,

But no one has started cooking dinner. I told
Ximena that we travel in the hope it will make us
Different, but I'm a bad tourist. Our friend Eduard
Showed us all the markets, the Hebrew inscription
In the Gothic Quarter, the recycled blocks of stone
From the Jewish graves on Montjuïc, the Roman walls
Of the old city, stone fountains empty from the drought.
In a narrow walkway in Raval, we passed

Bored prostitutes and junkies sniffing powder
Off the back of their hands. My feet and knees hurt
From walking, but I haven't changed. We saw
The square that was bombed by Mussolini's air force,
The shrapnel-torn walls, and the walls where
The ones who weren't fascists stood to be shot.
Some of the bullet holes were too high, and
I wondered if one of the executioners had

A bad conscience and fired above the skulls
Of his targets. I want to think so, but I'm not
Sentimental enough to believe it. In one of
The apartments, an air conditioner or a washing
Machine has stopped, and it's even quieter
Than before. Somewhere, water is draining
Down a pipe. Eduard also showed us the spot
On Rambla del Raval where a terrorist
Rammed his rented van into a crowd.

The van stopped on top of a Miró mosaic.
A few meters away, there's a Botero sculpture
Of a cat. Still, I'm a bad tourist. I don't know
What to make of what I see. The same dog
Continues to bark, and someone has put on
Some music I can barely hear. The sun has
Slipped behind the mountains.

"When Ximena is sad...."

When Ximena is sad,
The red anthurium fades to white,
The flags in front of schools
Hang drenched on their flagpoles,
And a burnt smell clings
To apartment hallways.

When Ximena is sad,
The dogs lie on their mats and stop
Barking at squirrels and strangers.
The black and white ducks
Take shelter under oak trees.
Clouds sink like a sudden frown
Above the cheekbones of sky and ocean.

When Ximena is sad,
The crows in her poems fly off the page,
Nest in the light fixtures, caw
From staircases. The fly who'd found
Heaven on an apple core buzzes
Hopelessly against the window.
The garbage chute refuses to open,
And the elevator on the right
Gets stuck on the 11th floor.

Ximena, don't be sad. The world
Is fragile and depends on you.

The Body Becomes More Beautiful as It Ages

Don't point out scars, wrinkles, or veins
Rising from the back of your hands. Even if
That were true, it's unimportant. As it ages,
The body ripens, becomes sweeter, calm—
Fingers touch differently, slowly, learning
Whatever can be learned from an arm
Or cheek, to know what *feeling* means,
That shiver arching your spine when my hand
Moves between your shoulder blades, down
Toward your waist. Our eyes are not guarded,
As they might have been when we were younger
And didn't understand what the world expected,
What we could give. Yesterday, we walked
Through a room of Rembrandt portraits and
Self-portraits, of faces that didn't flatter or resist
Age, but stared grimly back at us, visitors
Crowding the gallery looking for something
Beyond a lesson in art history. We wanted to meet
His eyes—so dark we could barely make them out—
To see what he had seen, and maybe we did.
We didn't discuss it. After dinner, we read,
As we often do, then turned off the lights
And held each other even more intensely
Than when we first met. Rembrandt painted
Himself just as time painted him, but the body
Isn't only decay and fever, the anxiety of creditors,
Poverty, and lawsuits from discarded lovers.
As it ages, the body ripens and becomes
More beautiful. As it ages, there is sweetness, calm.

Chinese Food and Polish Poets

Tonight, we went out for dinner at an ornate
Chinese restaurant, the kind of place with cocktails
As elaborate as the décor and paper umbrellas
Leaning against the glass. But, there on the menu
Were sea cucumbers in all their caterpillar-like
Glory. I thought immediately of Szymborska's
Poem "Autotomy," how when threatened,
The creature divides itself in two and abandons
Part of itself to the predator. Szymborska
Knew that doesn't work for us, that death
Doesn't leave some part of our being encased
In poetic glass. We're visiting my oldest son,
And I've brought with me Miłosz's anthology.*
Szymborska is in there with the rest—I think
They're all dead now. The anthology is their
Mausoleum and also their café, the place
Where their words meet, even if they're
No longer here to admire each other or
To disdain—I read somewhere that Miłosz
And Herbert had a falling out in their old age.
Does it matter? If they were holothurians,
Their arguments and grudges would be left behind,
Something for death to chew on, the way it
Takes everything else about us, our bodies,
Our skin, the air that comes out of our throats.
Miłosz believed that all things would be restored,
The meaning, perhaps, of heaven, a recognition
Of how perfect our lives were, even if we didn't
Know it. In his apartment in Poland, there
Was a bust of his wife who had died. He must
Have stared at her, wondering if she were waiting,
Looking back at their days and nights, gardening,
Planting annuals in pots with damp, black soil,
Picking caterpillars off their green leaves,
Caterpillars that look like small sea cucumbers.
But sea cucumbers don't make chrysalises
Or grow delicate wings. They break themselves
In two, in terror, unable even to realize what

Their deaths would mean. At the restaurant,
We ordered noodles and shredded chicken,
Salt-and-pepper shrimp and stir-fried green beans.
We saved the sea cucumber for another visit.

*Czeslaw Milosz. *Postwar Polish Poetry*. Univ of California Press, 8 July 1983

II. Soon, the Equilibrium Wobbled

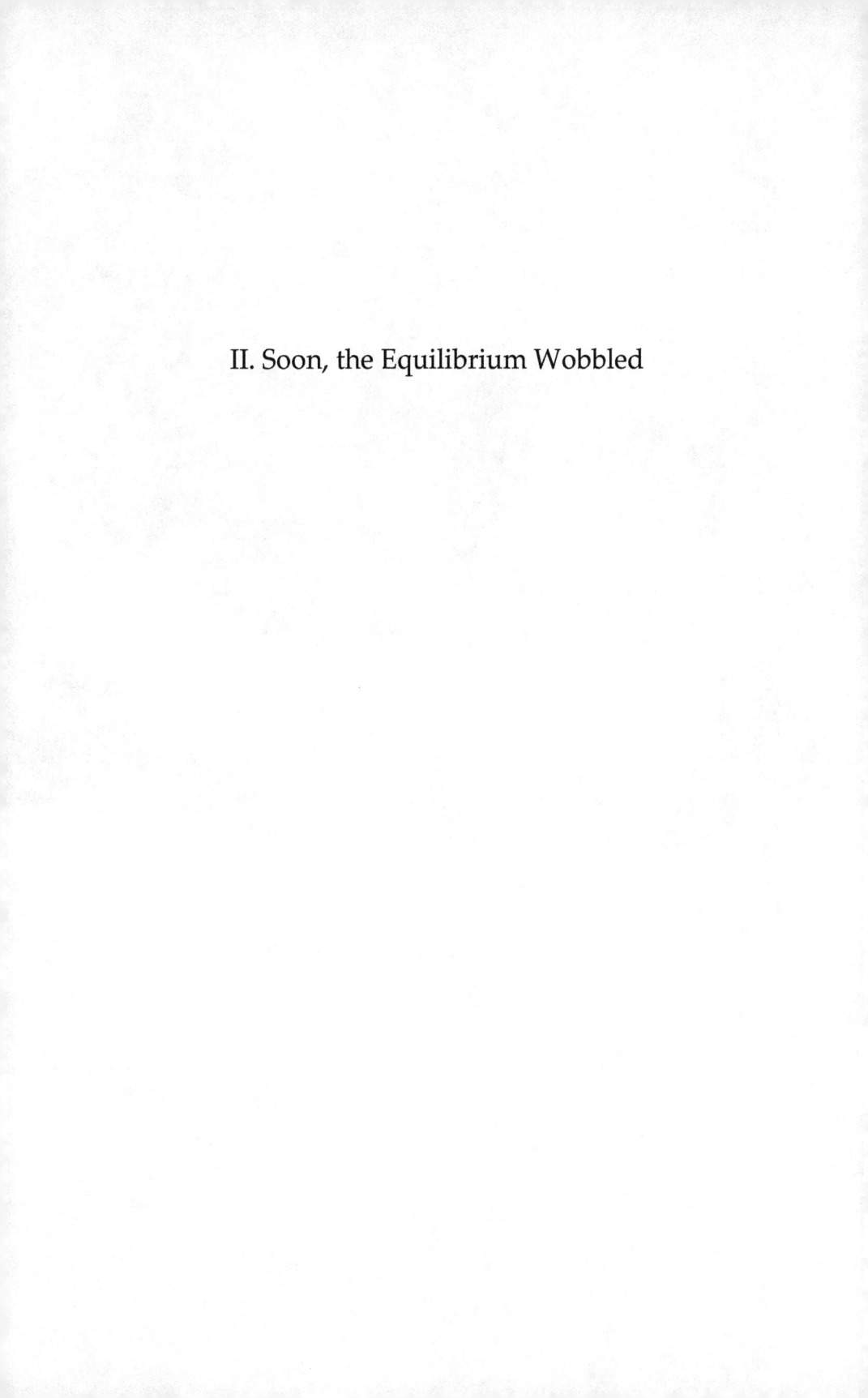

What's No Longer Here

My great aunt's egg-slicer, the table, benches
By the kitchen window, the crate filled with
Cantaloups that came in season from a valley
In West Texas—there was an enameled drip
Coffeemaker that waited so patiently on
The gas stove, the green can of Union Coffee
That opened with a key like a tin of sardines,
And when it rained, the smell of newspapers
Drying in the oven, and always the sound
Of ceiling fans, their paddles white propellers
Swirling the air above our heads.
All of this is gone. I may be the only
One left to remember it. Even the live oak
In the backyard, its wrinkled trunk too thick
To be encompassed by anyone's arms,
Was dug up to make way for a swimming pool
By the new owner, and next door, the bamboo
Forest was excavated for the same reason.
Later on, I lived in apartments, in cities,
In a rented farmhouse with a leaky basement
And mice that chewed their way through
The cereal boxes and the loaves of bread.
I don't know what happened to those places,
The wooden banisters that met my hand
Each morning, the radiators that were always
Too cold or too hot. People disappeared as well;
Marriages ended; friends died from old age,
Heart attacks, and disappointment. On Southern
Avenue, there was a warehouse where we bought
Dry ice for parties, clouds of carbon dioxide
Swirling in a punchbowl. The next morning,
The house smelled of cigarettes and bourbon.
The upholstery of the chairs and the blue couch
Held on to the stories my parents' friends
Told each other and to the sound of ice cubes
Rattling in glasses. Upstairs, in the rooms nobody
Used, the ivory-colored paint peeled
From the walls in long strips. It fell like

A weather event on the old suitcases and boxes
Of family papers. There are dictionaries
And paintings I still keep because, as Whitman—
Long vanished—would say, they remind me
Of myself. Tonight, when I fall asleep,
They also will disappear.

The Sulphur Match
—John Singer Sargent, 1882

I have no business being here, but neither does Sargent,
Sketching somewhere from across the room. The woman
With the red shawl leans back in her chair, her fingers

Touching the wall lightly, her chair resting on its hind legs.
Tonight, she wears her best shoes and tucks them up
Onto the crossbar of the chair. A wine bottle has rolled,

Empty, onto its side. How long did Sargent stare
At her and the man next to her? He lights a cigarette
With a sulphur match and wears a fur-collared cloak,

A black hat. At this moment, she is beautiful, but we
Don't know that the man sees more than a conquest,
That he sees what Sargent sees. The moment

May not last longer than the match.

My Grandfather's Chinese Vases

There was a story, I believe, behind each,
But no one ever told them to me. They
Presided over cabinets filed with books,
Leather-bound editions, and the blue
Carpets that were Chinese as well. My mother
Sold the carpets after he died, but we kept
Some of the vases, the one with layered glass,
And the oxblood one, the murky green,
And the cloisonné pair with dragons. My
Great-aunt had two yellow vases with
Phoenixes in mid-flight. She kept them
In a curio cabinet with miniature objects
Made of ivory or bone. The vases were
Small, and she was also. Childhood fevers
Had stunted her growth, left her unmarried,
Her evenings taken up with baseball on
The radio, cutting recipes out of the newspaper.
Like my grandfather, she left her false teeth
In a glass at night. In the morning, she'd
Put them back in and go downstairs to make
Coffee with chicory in a white enameled,
French-drip pot. When my grandfather died,
She moved in with us. My mother bought
Her a television for watching the games, but she
Was afraid to stay by herself if we went out.
There had always been someone to keep her
Company. She didn't like change. The Chinese
Vases were stored in the hall closet, along
With the crystal that was never used.

There Was a Pine Tree

If I have faith, it's that the world is sayable,
That I can find words for what I didn't think could be said.
The weight of a stone fountain filled with clear water,
The sunlight that plunges through vacant clouds,
Thoughts that are just images, faces, words spoken
Without meaning, the way one room in a dream becomes
Another, how it resembles the room I slept in at my
Grandfather's house, the deep red of the bricks,
The solidity of the white front door. There was a pine tree
In the front yard, and the sap thickened and dried
Between the shapeless tiles of bark, the smell of resin
That was left on my fingers, the infinity of acorns from
The live oak, the trunk that was older than anyone living
Who was not a tree. When my grandfather died, I didn't
Know what to believe. When my parents died
Thirty years later, it wasn't much different. I don't have
The talent for belief. Their voices only come to me
In snippets, in crumbling pieces of tree bark, in the odor
Of pine or the feel of acorns rolling in my hand.

What It Was Like to Grow Up During the Cold War

The brother of a girl in my class at school
Had long scabs across his legs where his father's
Belt connected with his calves. He was proud of
His punishment and showed it to anyone
Who would look. We were all eight or nine years old.
None of us had read Kafka, Nietzsche, or Freud.
We'd barely read Superman, The Green Lantern,
Or The Fantastic Four, and if the teachers
Noticed anything, they kept it to themselves.
His sister was a nice kid, did well at school.
His parents must have wished he was more like her.
On the playground, there was an obstacle course
Where you hung by your hands, swinging from bar to
Bar. I'd always fall—and I never made it
To the top of the climbing pole. The headlines
Were full of Sputnik, Castro, and Khrushchev's shoe
Banging against the table. When Kennedy
Was shot, the boy with the scabs ran down the hall,
Cheering until the teachers dragged him away.

Elsie and Alfred

I may be misremembering a lot of this. My parents
Told me nothing about the war until later, at least
The part about Hitler killing six million Jews,
Jews who could have been us, assimilated,
Pretending we were like everyone else in that
Southern city. I also hadn't learned yet about
The Christian kids at school whose parents didn't
Allow them to come to my house or invite me
To theirs or how it would feel when my third-grade
Teacher sat on a bench watching as my friend Steve
Started hitting me, repeating antisemitic rhymes
That didn't make sense. We lived in a neighborhood of
Old brick houses and streets lined with oak trees,
Not so different from streets in Germany or elsewhere.
Elsie and Alfred would come to visit my grandfather,
Who had helped pay the ransom to get them out,
Twenty or more years earlier. I remember them as
A frail couple, she, dressed in some kind of beige outfit,
Her husband narrow-shouldered, in a suit that seemed
Too large. They usually brought a cake Elsie had made,
One of my grandfather's favorites, and spoke in thick
Accents I could barely understand. My mother didn't
Like them much—I realized that. They were Jews
In a way we weren't. They were Jews who'd had to be
Rescued. They were not like her or me.

It's Yom Kippur, and I'm Not Fasting

The first thing I thought of this morning
Was coffee, café au lait in a
Blue ceramic bowl, a slice of toast
Still warm in my hand. I didn't even
Remember today was Yom Kippur.
I say I'm not observant, which sounds
Like I have poor eyesight but really
Means that when God and I have a chat
All I hear is a dial tone at
The other end of the line. I'm tired
Of imagining what doesn't have
An image. There're no burning bushes
In my backyard, just history that
Can't be changed, redeemed, or atoned for.
God, I have too many images
In my head today, videos of
Villages captured and recaptured,
Reporters asking, "Can you tell us
Where the bodies are buried?" Someone
Points to a field, fresh-turned dirt not far
From a road. Eighty-one years ago,
They were the bodies of Jews in a
Ravine in Kyiv, now Ukrainians.
When can we say atoning doesn't
Work? The Earth is full of graves, mass and
Singular. Trees send out roots to thread
Ribcages that insects and worms have
Already hollowed. Each year, the ground
Sinks a little. In the history
Of the world, no one ever went broke
Selling shovels. God, there is something
Wrong with people, and thousands of years
Of fasting hasn't fixed it. Neither
Has prayer or the sacrifice of
Unblemished cattle or first-born sons.
The sun will set soon, and the day will
Be over. I was taught the gates of
Heaven swing closed then: no more prayers.

The ones who haven't repented yet
Aren't going to. Another year's passed.
Men put on their jackets and walk home.

3 A.M.

It's 3 a.m., too late to start a poem,
Too late also to think about your mother
In the nursing home, her gray hair
Long, child-like, her arms bent close

To her chest, her body fetal in a hospital
Gown. You weren't there when she died,
But you watched your father as he
Went into arrest, heard the dust rattle

That came from his throat, a sound
Unlike any he'd ever spoken. Earlier
That day, he'd looked at you and said
He didn't understand why he had cancer.

He slipped between pain and morphine,
His liver failing, heart unable to keep up.
You told him you'd be staying, and that
Confused him too. A nurse woke you

At 1 or 1:30 to say, "He's dying."
You stood by the bed, watching.
It wasn't peaceful or holy. His body
Just stopped, like yours will, like your

Mother's did, like everyone's body has
Who's ever lived. And, he blamed you,
Probably until the end. His doctors had
Tried to tell him that colon surgery

Hadn't fixed the problem. The cancer
Was in his liver too. He wouldn't hear them,
So the doctors asked you to decide:
Curative or palliative? You chose palliative,

And took the blame. "You've killed me" —
His voice over the phone. "You were
The one who chose this." Now, when
You've finished cleaning up and are

Reading with only the dog for company,
They call for your attention, your mother
Who couldn't be moved from Louisiana
To Massachusetts and died alone, your

Father's bony face as the nurse closed
His eyes. Who are you to turn them
Away after all this time, even though
You're tired and it's too late to

Remember how they looked at you
Or their voices when they spoke? Who
Are you to turn them away, even
Though it's too late to write a poem?

Night Train to St. Louis

Crossing the Ozarks in the evening, we took
On trout to serve at dinner, with brown butter
And slivered almonds. My father had a highball,
My mother a coke. My grandfather drank iced tea.
Suitcases were large then, folded jackets
And ironed shirts, extra pairs of shoes, pajamas.
At night, I watched black fields and sky pass us
Going the other way. There was nothing remarkable
In any of this. The earth turned on its axis,
And the tracks, if I could have seen them, would've
Converged at infinity, a point visible to painters
And the very young. But I was not a painter, only
A pair of eyes sliding into sleep, a train
Pulling into a station, a few lights, many stars.

Obituaries

My mother used to say that only old people read them.
Now, I get an email about a classmate from high school,
Someone I might not have recognized over 50 years ago,
Much less today. I could call my friend Richard to ask,
Who was the guy who just died? And, Richard could tell me.
But the truth is that I don't want to keep track of acquaintances
Beneath the ground—or above it. The cemetery in Shreveport
Was just down the block from a drive-thru liquor store that
Didn't ask for IDs. The ability to turn the steering wheel and
Press the gas pedal was apparently good enough. On the same
Street, a fried chicken place sold onions pickled in jalapenos
And vinegar. They went down well with Jack Daniel's
On summer weekends when we'd play penny-ante poker
In someone's garage. Back then, almost none of us were dying.

Hollywood 1975

The summer we moved to LA, we didn't have air conditioning.
We'd rented an old adobe-colored garden apartment in Hollywood,
One that came complete with a busybody neighbor who'd look
At our black chow with his paws on the windowsill and mouth
Pulled back in a growl, a growl that meant he'd like nothing better
Than to give her a quick bite if he had the chance—she'd stare
First at him and then at me if I was nearby and tell him, "Poor baby,
You're like a little prisoner." If this especially ticked me off,
It was because I'd just spent weeks giving him meds, handfeeding him
Hamburgers, even carrying him downstairs and back up to a 2nd-floor
Motel room in Albuquerque when he needed to pee. He'd been hit
By a car, and for a few days, it hadn't looked good. But chows
Are nothing if not tough. He pulled through and eventually went back
To being his ornery self. The neighbor didn't know any of that.
I'd paid for the operation and treatment and didn't have much
Left for road trips. That was why I was in LA, working in a photo lab
And trying to train the dog to sit, heel, and not to run out in the street.
Monday through Friday, I spent almost all day in a darkroom,
Developing advertising photos, breathing chemicals labeled
Use only with proper ventilation, chatting about the stuff
People talk about to get through to 5:00: where to get burritos
With lots of cilantro or how the woman who just got fired had a kid
And really needed the work. *When they sent her home early, nobody
Said good-bye or wished her luck. We acted as though unemployment
Might be contagious.* At dinner, my wife told me, with enthusiasm,
That she'd applied for a job at a studio as a greens person—they're
The ones who move plants from one side of a sound stage to the other.
Mostly, they sit around, drink coffee, and smoke. Or at least they did then.
She told me she waited by the phone each day, but the studio never called.
Later, she let it slip she went to the beach with friends—
This was before cellphones—or drove on the freeway listening
To classical music. The car had air conditioning.

Reading The Classics

There was a used bookstore just above
86th Street—I don't remember
The name—where I overheard someone
Say the Greeks had no word for "success."
It was at a time in my life when
I didn't feel particularly
Successful. My marriage had become
(Don't lie—it always had been) a string
Of ugly fights. Each time, we wondered
If the words we'd said meant there was no
Going back, no forgetting this was
What we both really felt. The people
Who lived above us would comment through
The ventilation shafts, imitate
Our insults and laugh. They also liked
To play songs from *Camelot* and sing
Along. The woman next door received
Visitors, men who strangely brought bags
Of groceries. She'd put on music
With a loud bass, and I'd see them leave
Later when I went to walk the dog.
Her boyfriend waited outside, either
Sitting on the steps or in his car.
Eventually, they moved, and a
Korean family who'd bought the
Bodega on Columbus moved in.
I started taking Greek classes at
The New School. I remember the sun
Setting on Fifth Avenue in the
Summer, neon lights of restaurants
And bars, moments when the streets emptied,
When it felt good to walk to the class
Where we'd translate some lines of Plato,
Heraclitus, or Sophocles, and
Nobody mentioned the word "success."

Cambridge

My son tells me, "You wouldn't recognize Harvard Square,"
And I realize how much the details have faded, names disappeared,
Locations gone or fuzzy: the cafeteria with baked scrod and vegetables,
The place with good muffins and weak coffee served in dark brown cups,
The newspaper kiosk where I'd buy *The New York Times* on Sundays
And retreat to a below-street-level restaurant on Boylston where they'd
Let me sit for hours just for ordering a croissant or two, maybe
The ones with chocolate inside. When you're not yet twenty, you don't
Think about calories or cholesterol. Two brothers ran a bookstore
Right by the square, and one told a story about buying a first edition
Of *A Soldier's Pay* for a few dollars at a book sale, reselling it
For thousands. I never got that lucky at book sales, but I read a lot
And shuffled through the collapsed pile of poetry on the wooden table
By the couch at the *Grolier*. Gordon Cairnie, the owner, was alive then
And gossiped freely about the marriages of poets, but was oddly
Reluctant to recommend books. His only advice:
"They tell me William Butler Yeats was a pretty good poet."
I'd already bought my copy of Yeats, so I picked up Lawrence's
Selected Poems instead. Gordon didn't seem to mind. I think
He was surprised anyone purchased anything.

The Work of Grieving

Freud talks about the work of grieving, but
I've never really known how or even what
It feels like. I lost my grandfather, my
Great aunt, my father, mother, and friends
I knew for years. I went to their funerals,
And from time to time, wished they were here,
Wished I could tell them a story about something
I saw or did. For some reason, it never occurred
To me that they might be interested in politics
Or the evening news, which says something,
I'm sure, about how shallow I am. I can
Read how Walter Benjamin killed himself
When it looked like he'd be turned back
To France, handed over to the Nazis, and
The thought of it makes me want to cry. Stories
From the Cambodian genocide affect me
The same way. But I didn't cry for my grandfather
Or anyone else except two dogs the vet killed
Because they were ill with no hope of getting better.
Half the people I knew in college aren't
In reunion pictures anymore. The old photos
Show them with hairstyles and clothes
From the 1970s, and the newer ones show them—
Or at least some do—with gray hair and t-shirts
That look out of place, old men dressed up
In motorcycle jackets. There are women who
Were still girls when I knew them, who disappeared
Without a word from me or from them,
But I haven't grieved anyone. All I can do
Is think about their names, and occasionally,
Take a look at some pictures.   When I disappear
As they have, don't feel you have to mourn me.
I haven't grieved anyone.

How One Thing Might Lead to Another

What does it matter if I tell you I wanted something more? The yellow,
Finch-like bird up in the branches—I can't name him, and if I'm honest,
The tree itself escapes me. Is it a beech? I could take a photo and try

To figure it out, but by then, it'll be too late. The moment will have gone
Wherever time goes when it's no longer where it was, where I am too,
Until I'm somewhere else. I remember the pine trees at my grandfather's

House, the oak tree that was older than the streets that surrounded it,
The pecan that would throw down each fall those smooth, pointy-ended
Nuts. Even though I didn't like them much, I'd gather buckets just

Because it didn't seem right to turn down a gift. I think my parents
Were happy, at least some of the time. They'd both been surprised
By what they'd been given. My father, an orphan, married my mother's

Family as much as he'd married her, and my mother finally loved
In middle age and gave birth. Her friends had all married at least ten years
Before. They met for bridge on Wednesdays and gossiped appropriately.

There was an equilibrium. My father traveled then, wholesaling women's
Shoes. It was a life of hotel rooms and badly cooked food, but he liked it.
Later, he'd become a stockbroker and stay in one place. His office

Smelled of ink from the teletype machine, rolls of paper, and ashtrays,
Crushed cigarettes, shreds of tobacco. He never liked hiring and firing,
Especially firing. I inherited that. Soon, the equilibrium wobbled.

My grandmother died, my grandfather, my great aunt who lived with us.
There was a war in Vietnam, and the world shrunk to fit inside
A black-and-white TV. Kennedy was assassinated, and Walter Cronkite

Almost became a member of the family. I read National Geographics
And imagined myself in France or Italy. I'd need a good sweater, a pair
Of shoes with thick soles for walking. As soon as you want something

More than you've got, the equilibrium is lost. Maybe, it's already lost
And you just don't know it. My father died of colon cancer and my
Mother from dementia. The roof of the house was rotting by the time

It was sold. I gave away the National Geographics.

Among Magnolias

I waited among magnolias in Louisiana with dark green leaves and
 heavy white blossoms, on August nights thick with humidity,
 drinking beer in someone's driveway,
I waited breathing air that tasted wet, the headlights of cars, of
 sedans, convertibles, station wagons, speeding down Line
 Avenue past my window,
Or waited with friends, passing joints, sitting on the hood of a
 Pontiac out by the airport fence, planes landing over our heads—
Just another sentimental story of adolescence and loss. I left
 Shreveport at 16, then left it again at 17. There was no
 guidebook for leaving. I went all the way to New Hampshire.
In below zero weather in Franconia, it was hard to feel my nose. I
 waited for the envelope with my Vietnam lottery number—I
 knew already I wouldn't make a good soldier—but my number
 was high enough never to be called. I didn't think much about
 what happened to the guys whose numbers were lower.
In Europe, I waited in hotel lobbies reading *The Herald Tribune* to feel
 less lonely. It didn't work.
In my marriage, I waited too. Even then, I didn't feel less lonely and
 didn't know what I wanted.
I didn't know that loneliness has its own language—impossible to
 learn, full of rules that don't make sense—with only one
 pronoun.
I didn't know that if you let loneliness bother you long enough it
 might turn into solitude, and you might write a poem about
 what you want and what you don't have.
Of course, it would be a bad poem, one of those sentimental stories
 of adolescence and loss, but it might make you feel the loneliness
 less or feel there's a purpose to it.
Now, I count all the places I waited, the B&Bs in London, the
 apartments in New York and Boston, freeways in LA that lead to
 the ocean, the checkerboard of streets that run to the Everglades
 in Miami,
And I know that loneliness has no purpose, and cafés are better for
 waiting than hotel lobbies—I don't think they publish *The Herald
 Tribune* anymore.

Written on Boxing Day

I've never been to London this time of year,
Though I remember a cold night staying
At a hostel there once, an old guy in
The next cubicle (no private rooms)
Hacking a lifetime of cigarettes out
From his lungs. I left the next day by train
For Edinburgh, a room above a bar and
Down the street from a brewery. In
The morning, the air outside smelled of
Fermenting grain, and at night, inside,
The noise of the customers and the singer
Who covered Dusty Springfield songs
Shook the floorboards. I was eighteen
And had no idea what I was doing there
Or anywhere else. I bought oranges and
Chestnuts and read all day, only going out
For meals or books—spy novels, poetry,
The occasional memoir. I wanted, I think,
To unmake myself, become someone
I'd actually want to know, someone who
Wasn't waiting for something to happen to him,
A sudden romance or shattering revelation.
Of course, neither happened. I don't mean
There weren't moments: in Paris, the Assyrian
Sculptures in the basement of the Louvre, in
The morning when no one else was there—
They were more real than I was. I could
Understand why they'd been worshiped—
Beards, wings, split hooves for feet,
Expressionless faces that never answered
Prayers. They offered nothing except their own
Existence. Then there was the Gauguin exhibit
At l'Orangerie, but I was too young to think of him
As someone else who didn't know what he wanted
Or where he belonged. Back in the States,
I spent the next Christmas with a college girlfriend
And her family in Flatbush. They were Methodists
And expected me to go to church with them. I

Don't remember what they did, if anything,
For Boxing Day, but by the spring semester,
We weren't together anymore.

Commuting

Those were the years I lived in Ossining,
Taking the train into Manhattan to teach
At Lincoln Center, stopping at the bakery
In Grand Central for my three chocolate
Muffins and an enormous coffee. That's
What got me through the day at Fordham.
I'd think about it waiting on the platform
For the Amtrak to the city, the wind blowing
Off the river, clouds looking like it'd snow
Before noon. There was a priest who'd
Take the same train. He'd worked in
El Salvador and buried a lot of people.
After a few conversations, I asked him
About it, how he could handle so much
Death. He was matter of fact:
"Everybody dies." I didn't know if
It was really that simple, or if this
Was a practiced answer, if others like me
Had asked him the same thing. I gave
My classes Whitman and Christina Rossetti,
Short stories by Lawrence and Borges.
I learned to fold the newspaper the way
Only New York commuters know how to do.
Going home, the train pushed quickly
Through the Bronx and up to Westchester,
Smelling of diesel and exhaustion.

Sleeping Dogs

I'm tired of writing about what's no
Longer here, the sun rising over
A parking lot in Cambridge, the dog
Chewing the doorframe whenever we
Left him alone, a black male chow with
Attachment issues, a fear-biter
Who had to be tied to a cage door
To be examined by a vet. I
Used to dream about him long after
He died from kidney problems. This is
What I mean: what more is there to say
About him, about that empty space
In my twenties, the marriage where we
Fought across multiple states, the chow
Left in the car with the windows cracked
While we ate at a truck stop? He ripped
Deep holes in the back seat, a message
About exclusion and being on
The wrong side of a revolution.
He used to jump through closed windows when
He'd see a squirrel outside, leaving
Broken glass all over but somehow
Not getting cut himself. The squirrels
Always got away. Just because I
Still think about it doesn't make it
Important or a metaphor for
A marriage where we blamed each other
For every disappointment. Once in
That apartment in Cambridge, he was
Chasing something in his sleep, his legs
Kicking—barks, growls from between his teeth.
My wife tried to wake him. His head turned.
He bit her—not hard, but enough to
Make her cry out and run for the door.
He chased her, waking up somewhere in
The living room. There was no squirrel
Or neighbor's cat. Whatever it was
Had gotten away. For two days, we talked
About having the vet put him down—
Finally decided against it.

A Persistent Roar

In Massachusetts, our building faced an alley
Behind some grad student housing.
When it snowed, they plowed us last,
And when they did, the plow would dump
Mounds of snow on top of the cars, the hard
Heavy stuff that turns to concrete by the time
You can get down to shovel it off. Just across
The alley was a commercial laundry.
The extraction cycle shook the whole building.
You didn't put anything on the edge of a table.
In the spring, though, I'd leave to go camping,
By myself, in New Hampshire or Vermont.
My wife stayed behind, preferring
Regular showers and time on her own. Things
Were not good between us. One year, I left
Too early, and I wandered onto a trail that had been
Washed out by flooding. I had to cross a stream
That was above my thighs, and I came out shaking,
My body temperature lower than it should be.
It was still daylight, but I crawled into my sleeping bag
To get warm. When I woke up the sun had already
Dropped below the mountains. I cooked oatmeal
On a brass camping stove and went back to sleep.
Two divorces later, I don't remember the things
We fought about then or why they were important,
But I remember the smell of oatmeal, the stars sliding
West, and the persistent roar of that stream.

Fingermarks

On a day in July, I threw clothes
Into a green plastic garbage bag.
My computer and monitor were
Already in the trunk. A few books
Were tossed in with the clothes, and papers
Were sticking out from my pockets. I
Moved quickly, but not quickly enough.
My wife blocked the doorway, refusing
To let me pass, make it to the car.
When I tried to push past her arm, she
Grabbed my throat with both hands. Whatever
She was screaming I don't remember.
Her fingermarks were still on my neck
When I checked into an old motel
By the Charles River. There was a beige
Phone and a curtained window that looked
Out on a highway, a liquor store,
And the white lines of a parking lot.
I stared at the phone for a long time.

Against Elegy

> *The meaning of anything is merely*
> *other words for the same thing.*
> —Charlie Chaplin, *Limelight*

I miss your presence in this world, and I call
That feeling *loss*, which only means *I*
Miss your presence in this world. Death

Is stupid, and loss is just as bad.
Would I feel better if your absence
Were heroic or sacrificial? If there were

Some purpose to it? There wasn't.
A little spot of thickened blood
Slid almost randomly into an artery,

And everything came to a stop. It had
Nothing to do with your life or mine
Or anything you wanted to accomplish.

It wouldn't have mattered if you'd died
For some worthy cause. I'd still miss you
And have no words to encompass

What I felt. Metaphor's inadequate,
And even worse, seems false. You don't
Hover in my thoughts. You haven't

Moved to another country, a place where
You could receive phone calls, exchange
Text messages. You're not swooping around,

An unseen bird or Amazon delivery drone,
Checking out everything going on below.
You're already ashes and memories that

Aren't dimming as quickly as they should.
I can't think of any worse fate for you
Than watching us, your friends, from up

In some cloudy heaven, seeing us make
Mistakes you would have prevented,
Forgetting what you would have remembered.

I'd like to think you died out of
Frustration with people who couldn't
See the obvious. You could've seen it,

Did see it, but now you can't. Death might
Be a relief after that kind of rage.
Except it isn't. The only you that's left

Is the one I carry around complaining
In my head. If other people carry you around
The same way, that's someone different,

Someone they knew, not me. You don't have
To remind me that language falters,
Confronted by what doesn't exist. It

Can signify but not describe, which is why
We make shit up. Even Homer does it,
Imagining Achilles wandering around

Those sunless lands, remembering the bright
World he left behind. It's so much worse
Than that. You're not a spirit in Hades's

Fields. You're not even you. You're gone,
Become nothing, and I'm left with nothing to
Say or imagine, just a handful of words that

Don't mean much of anything.

In Florida We Don't Have Mountains

In Florida we don't have mountains, barely hills.
It surprises me water flows to the ocean
Here at all. I think of it resting without tension,

Stagnant, the odor of those green landfills
Casting shadows on the highway. You
Roll up your windows, as you drive to
Orlando, housing developments rising

Just across the road—where they probably don't
Smell it anymore, vents releasing
Fumes that seep into clothes, that haunt

Clear skies at night or dawn, the view
To the east, grass cut by tractors weekly,
Men in masks driving across the slopes,
Emerald-green mounds, shockingly perfect.

Sunday Morning

Waking up from a dream about a torturer, who looked like an actor whose name I can never remember—in the movies he played gangsters and crooked politicians. I'm not particularly heroic in my dreams, but in this one I told him, or maybe just thought, "This is the only way you can express love." I never got to hear his reply, which probably wouldn't have been particularly reassuring. Instead, I rolled toward the clock by my bed and opened my eyes enough to see I'd slept longer than I planned. I pressed my lips against your shoulders and your neck, your skin smelling faintly of soap and sweat. You stirred in your sleep but didn't wake, having better dreams, I hope, than mine.

A Normal Life

I am who I am. It's probably too late
To change or pretend to change. These backyard
Shadows cast against a wooden fence
Remind me of Sorolla, his paintings filled
With light and foliage, an afternoon sliding
Into evening. It's a good thing I don't
Take history personally. Otherwise, I'd
Find it cruel to lose a country at an age
When friends die of heart attacks before I
Learn they're sick. *When I say "lose,"*
I mean it's a country that doesn't feel like
Mine anymore. And those persistent ads
From online gun shops—they make me think
My neighbors are stocking up for some
Climactic shootout with brown-skinned
Gangs of *sicarios* or some other movie fantasy.
Still, we wave to each other when I walk my dog
And they walk theirs, and we say hello
At the supermarket, realizing our shopping carts
Contain the same flour, chicken, coffee, and fruit.
I try not to imagine the excuses we'll use later
To keep up the appearance of a normal life.
Last year, I sat in the garden of Sorolla's
House in Madrid, the light tinted by camellia
Blossoms, the shadows by dark green leaves.
The dictatorship there lasted almost half
A lifetime, thirty-six years if you're counting.
In Barcelona, we saw the pastry shop
Where Franco ate. I don't know which
Pastries he chose—I hope not the same ones
I did. We tell ourselves that politics is
Unavoidable but untrustworthy. Only time
Is a reliable ally. Dictators get old and
Choke on their pastries. The understudies
Who wait offstage grow impatient, their

Lines already memorized. Young officers
Preen their feathers in front of the mirror
And think how tired they are of saluting.
One aging senator tells an embarrassing
Anecdote about another, one too many times.
Meanwhile, the days, like senile relatives,
Repeat the same stories, and we console
Each other, impotently, so impotently,
Telling those same repeated stories,
painted shadows and camellia blossoms,
Dark green foliage blocking the light.

Hawaii, 1968

When we folded up the ground cloths in the morning, sometimes there'd be a centipede or two who'd burrowed through the sand at night for the warmth, the enormous black sky having pulled the heat out of the rocks and vegetation. We'd stare up at the white dust of the Milky Way and point to Orion, visible even this far south, while our own bodies glowed beneath our sleeping bags and tarps, and the centipedes with their poisonous bites basked in the unexpected warmth. Later, I met a woman who'd been bitten, her arm swollen, discolored, still hurting, and after that, I'd sleep whenever I could on top of picnic tables or benches, imagining my body heat wasted, drifting up like steam, and half-frozen centipedes barely moving in the dark.

*

I don't remember now whether the airport was on Maui or the Big Island, but we had a flight early the next morning and decided to sleep on the gray-carpeted floor in the departure lounge. The guards told us we could stay there but only if we didn't lie down or close our eyes. It didn't make sense, but guys with uniforms and holsters on their belts rarely say things that do. I was fourteen, and I knew that already. The rest, I was still trying to figure out. I had two paperbacks with me, the Dhammapada and Tolstoy's Essays on Civil Disobedience. I realize now that both were about how the world didn't make sense the way everybody said it did. Somewhere around 4 or 5 a.m., the newspapers were delivered. Soviet tanks had crossed into Czechoslovakia. The Prague Spring hadn't lasted through August. I was in a small airport in Hawaii, waiting to check my bicycle and board a plane. In Prague, the protestors were blocking streets with their bodies.

Seven Mile Bridge

How much sorrow does it take to fill a gas tank,
To get in the car and drive south to the Keys,

Where land stops and the sea writes epitaphs
In the sand each morning, stretching the horizon

To a fold of blue paper? It's not the dying that's
So hard. It's leaving all that behind. I had

A client a few years back, a *machista* who came on
To any woman he met. We'd talked over coffee a week

Before I got the text. He—I won't use his name—
Was just out of the hospital, waiting for a transplant.

He was thin and said the strokes made it hard
To remember, but he still stopped a woman going by,

Joked about the dog she was walking, made her
Laugh. He needed to go back to court, modify

Child support because he wasn't making any money.
His hair was dark, not dyed, and he didn't look old.

But the skin had hardened and collapsed around
His eyes. He knew he wasn't what he had been,

What he still wanted to be. There's no reaching
A deal with loss. You just get in the car and drive.

Dog Years

Tomorrow, I'll get up early to drive
The dog to the vet. He's having the rest
Of his teeth removed. They're decayed,
And he gets gum infections. He bleeds
From his mouth, and his breath smells like
Something that's been dead for a while.
There's a hernia too—none of it's good.
Ximena asked what he'll eat afterwards.
I told her "The same food. Dogs don't
Really chew; they mostly swallow."
This one, named after Joseph Brodsky, is
Nine years old, which for a collie is getting
Up there. The collie who slept in my
Room when I was growing up—or slept in
My parents' room—only lived to be twelve.
I was away at a high-school debate workshop
When they called me to say they'd had him
"Put down." I was speaking from a wooden
Phone booth at a college in Texas, and I
Remember the grain of the wood. We have
Lots of euphemisms about killing dogs. I
Think I hate every one of them. When the vet
Gave my doberman an injection that stopped
His heart, I was still young enough not to
Imagine myself like him, unable to walk,
A cancer growing down my spine. Now, it's
All too easy to picture: the cold metal of
A raised examination table, the professionally
Sad look of the veterinarian as her syringe
Empties into my vein, maybe the distant
Sound of somebody crying, a receptionist
Mumbling under her breath, something
About the "rainbow bridge."

Song of a Prospective Exile

I'd have to leave so much behind, the library
That kept me company growing up, the art books
I favored at puberty, stories by Robert Louis Stevenson,
My 19th century edition of Whitman, my Dickens,
Jonathan Swift, and the Aesop's Fables with Hollar's
Illustrations—my mother repaired the backing
With scotch tape—all the cookbooks and dictionaries,
And the poets, philosophers, the novels in piles
On my night table. Where would they go?

I've seen books before in dumpsters. It's ugly.
If a Torah falls to the ground, the one who dropped it
Fasts for 40 days. If these books are pulped, no one may care.
The paintings? The portrait of my grandmother and my mother
As a child? It won't go with me. Or the Dutch interior,
Or the vases and china. Or the calligraphy that Korean abbot
Wrote for me so many years ago. For sure, I'd have to
Leave them all anyway. Nothing goes with us when we die.
Somehow, that's easier to accept. It feels natural.
This isn't. When you came from Colombia, you brought
A suitcase and a few mementos, a silver tray, Borges,
And Freud. No one imagines leaving twice, but we
Both know people who have. Kelly and her family, who
Left Castro in Cuba and then Chavez in Venezuela—
There are others.

           When I taught poetry classes at Fordham,
I had students who'd fled Hitler, remembered pogroms
During the Pilsudski Republic. When Jessie Jackson
Called New York "Hymietown," one declared,
"I left one country; I can leave another." There was
An actress from the Yiddish theater, who'd studied
At the Moscow Arts—how many borders had she crossed?
They all abandoned so much. I think of our friends
Francisco and Flor, who moved to Sevilla. They'd left
Nicaragua before and could sense a change here.

Where would I go, carrying some clothes and a laptop?
What country wants someone who only brings with him

A few poems he's memorized? Oedipus, blinded, traveled
With Antigone and Ismene looking for a place to die. Today,
Oedipus is everywhere, and no one wants to take him in.
Brecht claimed to have changed his country more often
Than his shoes. How many pairs did he abandon?
How many apartment doors did he lock and leave
The key in the mailbox? I studied with Brodsky after
The Soviets put him on a plane for Vienna. He left his
Parents, the rooms where he grew up, his Russian language.

He had us memorize Thomas Hardy, Frost, and Auden—
Maybe so we'd have poems to take with us if we
Ever had to get on a plane and leave the U.S. Each day,
The news gets worse, but the truth is, I don't want to go
Anywhere. I don't want to leave my family, friends,
This cramped townhouse filled with bookshelves and
This dining room table where I sit to write, where we've
Eaten and talked so often over coffee. I don't want to leave
The shape of these words that my tongue and lips know
Already how to form, that float easily on my breath.

Each day, the news gets worse, the detention centers
More numerous, the line of deportees longer. Even though
You're a citizen, you ask me what I'd do if you had to leave,
Go back to Colombia, a small apartment in Cali or Bogotá,
Taking only clothes and the poems you carry in your head,
And I tell you I'd go with you. I don't want to leave,
But I would.

Not All That Far From Lincoln Center

The chairs in the laundromat were orange and made of plastic,
Probably so no one would want to steal them. It was either the late 70s
Or the early 80s, not sure which, but I suppose I needed clean clothes
And walked up toward Broadway with a load. I didn't know Pavarotti
Was singing at the Met that Sunday afternoon and didn't know
The owner of the laundromat was Argentinean and loved opera.
He had a small, black-and-white television plugged into an outlet,
The rabbit-ears pulled first one way and then the opposite,
The volume turned up all the way, Pavarotti doing that thing of his
Where he'd stand on tiptoes to get a note. *I'm not sure
Why that helped, but I'm not a singer.* The drums of the dryers
Rotated loudly, the metal buttons on some blue jeans knocked
Against the ribs of the machine. Somebody's wet towels banged
As their washer went into the spin cycle. Pavarotti sang "Nessun Dorma"
For an encore, but on the screen, the singer was barely visible
For what we used to call "snow," the reception blocked by thick walls
And, beyond those walls, apartment buildings and offices.
We had to listen even harder.

A Question for Borges

He wore a blue suit and his hands steadied a mahogany cane
As he sat with a straight back, staring toward the audience.
It was a large room, somewhere in the library. The students
Were down front, the rest of us crowded in wherever
We could find a seat. I'd hoped to hear him recite poems,
But there wasn't much of that, just an interview,
His translator, and the room uncomfortably warm.
When they asked for questions from the audience,
I held my hand up, unsuccessfully. Instead,
A woman asked him about Donald Trump
And the Westway Project. (This is a true story.)
He apologized and turned his head toward his
Translator. He knew nothing about either.
I held my hand up again, but the translator
Called on someone else. I wanted to ask about
Nietzsche and eternal repetition. Was it just a literary device,
Or did he think we'd come back to this room in Manhattan,
Walk a second time the steps to the library? On the other side
Of the campus, would Lipchitz sculpt again *Bellerophon
Taming Pegasus*, black figures crashing through space? I thought
It was a good question, but I was wrong. It was better
The translator called on someone else. I was a belated adolescent,
Asking the question only to show how closely I'd read,
How much the work meant to me. Now, I'm almost as old
As Borges was then, that afternoon at Columbia. I know
That nothing is just a literary device, and it doesn't matter
Whether writers believe their own fictions. The Borges
Who answered questions and shrugged when he thought
They were unintelligible was not the same man as the one who
Wrote "*La noche cíclica*," but he wasn't a different man either.
We take the words as written. The room in the library,
The woman asking about Westway, Bellerophon, Pegasus,
Olympus distant and unattainable—they all are happening again,
Right now, and the blind poet shrugging at the questions
As though he were someone else, another Borges who,
Also blind, had wandered onto the stage by mistake,
He continues to stare at the audience, to hold his mahogany cane,
To try courteously to answer.

III. To Be Alive in Someone Else's Skin

A Man Made of Stories

Where to begin? The tips of his fingers, his toenails?
Each could tell you about the war, about his family, the uncle

Whose body was never found, the letter a woman wrote to him afterwards,
Thinking her child might be his. No one sent her an answer, even
To tell her he was probably dead. The palms of the hands: smooth but

With lines a fortune teller could spend hours interpreting, the love line
Filled with interruptions, infidelities—his own and those of others—

The life line surrounded by lines of protection, good luck, an old age
Without deprivation. The mound of Venus was large and fleshy.
He was passionate, and women had desired him. There was a scar

On his knee where he fell as a child and another on his forehead, half-
Hidden by his hair, a war wound from a fight with neighboring kids,

The armies on opposite sides of a fence. He'd climbed it and got a stick
Thrust at his eye for his trouble. It just missed. As a teenager,
He'd slouched in the park with friends at night, smoked marijuana

And drank bad wine. The sticky taste still hides somewhere
On the roof of his mouth. His tongue avoids it. His nose has changed

As he's gotten older. Each office where he worked had a different smell,
Desks where others had typed, left aspirin in the right-hand drawer. Their
Bodies had molded the chair back. Oil from the hair of other men made

Shiny the top edge of the chair. Had they fallen asleep when
No one was looking, as he had? His nose remembered the astringent

Smell of hair tonic and the smell of the disinfectant they used on
The bathroom floors. (He never called it a restroom.) His ears
Recalled a man coughing two stalls away, the toilet's flush, the water

At the sink. There was a small mole on his arm in the exact
Same spot where his father had such a mole. He spent his life afraid

He would become his father, frustrated, impatient, disappointed in himself,
Eager for the approval of others. Luckily, his eyes were different. His father
Had blue eyes; his were brown. But their hair was similar, thinning as he aged.

Each pore of his skin seemed to him like a well, one that could swallow him
And from which he'd never climb out. He looked at himself in the mirror,

Examining that spot between his nostrils and his cheek. To him, it was an
Alien planet. Whiskers grew nearby. He shaved them, but each morning they
Returned, just to spite him. Each had a story of its own.

The House in Louisiana

Memory's a landscape, camellias and a greenhouse
With orchids. His parents' house, first white, then
Painted pink by his mother—people called it

"The pink house"—and he remembers the canopy
Of oak trees over the street, the Japanese magnolia

By his window. There was a rose bed at the kitchen door,
Azaleas and lilies by the driveway. *His mother was losing
Her sight, but could still see color.* From half a continent away,

He can find the location on a map, the corner house,
No longer pink, the street named after a lake, the bricks solid

As the future they'd all been promised. A hundred years ago,
There were parties on the flat roof, dancing, colored lights,
Drinks during prohibition. There're no pictures of the house from then.

He regrets that. He imagines silver trays with champagne glasses,
Hors d'oeuvres, passed by white-gloved hands hired for the occasion,

Eyes observing everything—discretely. Behind the house,
There was a grass-covered alley that ran between painted
Brick walls and high fences. The village policeman had shot

A prowler in that alley sometime before the First World War.
No one questioned it or talked about how it happened. He always

Expected to see a ghost there, but never did. There'd been
Arched French doors on the front porch, but they were
Replaced with metal screens to keep out mosquitos. Red stone

Tile sank away from the house. Steps led to a portico.
He'd taught himself to ride a bike under that portico, hidden

Where no one could see him fail. He pushed down hard on the pedal
With one foot and tried to push with the other before he fell. Eventually,
He rode off, up the street. The house stayed where it was.

Even the Gods Die

Even the gods die, some heroically,
Fighting with axes, swords, spears,
Some sailing off into nothingness,
Their eyes cloudy and pale.
If they were not dead, we couldn't
Build highways and cities. They would
Always stand invisible on the walls,
Urge us to assemble a fleet to avenge
Some slight or theft by tribes from the east,
The south, warriors who wear pants
Like women, the way the Persians did.
If they were not dead, oil tankers
Would not cross the Strait of Hormuz, and
Satellites wouldn't pass overhead at night
Like stars that have lost their way in the dark.
Whatever the legends say, they don't return.
There are no sounds of footsteps on
Mount Olympus. Hephaestus's forge
Stands covered in ice. If Aphrodite wanted
Ares, her husband would not leap up
To stop her, but she's gone as well,
Perhaps beneath the ocean's waves or
The gaping earth. You will say that
New gods replaced them, and I'll nod
So as not to offend you. But, we both know
How hard it is to believe the stories.
Zeus was easy to picture, a swan or white
Bull, gold raining down on a princess.
Men burned cattle on his altars. What
Do you sacrifice now? Who receives
Your prayers, your confessions of fault?
The old gods would have laughed
At the spectacle. They did not require
Belief or good deeds. They loved the rogues
They'd punish for eternity, ones who'd push
Great stones pointlessly uphill or stand before
Banquets that couldn't be touched. You say
Your new gods cannot be seen, existing

Beyond us, beyond the stories. How do you
Know these gods are not dead as well,
Their tombs also beyond us, beyond
The stories? Perhaps you're right not to listen
To my blasphemy. Who knows what penance
Might be imposed on you, how many stars
And planets you would have to count, or
What filthy stables you'd have to clean?
The gods lasted a long time on their mountains,
In their banquet halls, their chariots pulled
By horses across the sky. But they've vanished
And taken your new gods with them. Airplanes
Cross above the mountains and oceans.
There are no more chariots or prophets lifted
Up to heaven. We cannot bring them back
Or pretend they hide behind the clouds.
They fell asleep, and the earth covered them.
Mounds of dirt and grass conceal their decay.
They have no families to weep for them,
No lovers or friends, and no one worships
Gods they know are dead. It's sad to think of it.
But if the gods were not dead, if they woke
For a moment, they'd despise most those
Who'd turn them into ideas or flimsy
Spirits who don't change or desire. Give us,
They'd say, the dignity of our death, of
A sky that is only sky and an earth that's
Only earth, with nothing beyond us now
And nothing beyond the stories.

Without a Soul

People who have souls, I guess, are lucky,
But I'm not one of them. Cut me open,
And no shimmer of invisible self
Will fly off to heaven or sink to hell
Or drift, a lost weather balloon across
The stratosphere. Inside of me, there's not
Another me, a less-tangible gust
Of stubborn opinions, drafts of poems,
And fondness for garlic. What you see is
Probably all you'll find, the old guy on
The autopsy table, dull eyed as a
Supermarket trout packed in melting ice.

A friend, the other day, told me I was
A materialist. Maybe he's right,
But I do believe in desire. It flows
Beneath our skin, a wind, ephemeral,
Unseen, eager, and utterly mortal.
People who have souls may be lucky, but
Those without may be luckier. I think
About all the nights we've held each other,
How I wake the next morning, my lips pressed
To your neck, shoulders, resting my hand on
Your thigh, listening to my own heartbeat,
Listening to your breath on the pillow.

On those mornings, our bodies are enough.

In Heaven

In heaven, Goya's no longer deaf. He hears
Everything Velázquez tells him when they sit
Together in one of those gardens the angels

Maintain for the blessed who care more
For conversation and deep-colored roses
Than for divinity. Velázquez is sad.

There are no dogs to paint or war horses
Or deer with magnificent antlers.
He tells Goya, "Only you can understand me."

Eternity is a difficult adjustment
For beings who're used to days and nights,
Beginnings, endings. Velázquez

Says, "What I painted is fixed in time,
An Infanta who will never age, royalty
On horseback, dwarves who saw everything

And said nothing." Goya: "My portrait
Of Altamira's red-suited child, the cats ready
To leap on his birds—time runs like water

Through our hands. Only the living
Have such moments. In this garden, roses
Never wilt, and weather's neither too

Cool nor too hot." An angel, who's been
Adjusting God's voluminous robes,
Flies past, but not a leaf sways from

The pulsing of his wings. "My friend,"
Says Velásquez, "sometimes I do not
Believe we are in heaven."

The Unfinished Golem

Inside these sentences is a cave.
Inside the cave is the skeleton
Of a man. His bones are carved from words.
His arms and legs phrases, sharp twisted
Wire and syllables. The cave is dark
And the stiff bones shiver even though
There's no wind. Meyrink might recognize
Him as a golem, perhaps one left
Unfinished, the secret name never
Inscribed on his forehead, a golem
Who never took his first steps or stood
Guard over his maker's sad prayers.

The skeleton is missing teeth, hands,
Parts of a clavicle. Loneliness
Has burrowed into his tibia.
He has no ankle—or companion.
He is not Adam, and God hasn't
Formed his mate from a remaining rib.
There is no mercy in words, at least
None for creatures who only exist
In sentences, and lack tongue to
Rise to grammar or comprehension.
Reader, do not withhold your pity
From bones that have never been alive.

Wisława Szymborska and the Wounded Angel

A Polish poet was taking her exam on the History of Humanity.
It was still winter, but the first snowdrops had pushed
Their way through the hard earth. The grass was still brown,
But there were bushes with leaves. Inside, a pencil scratched
Stubbornly against a sheet of cheap paper. The questions
On the exam were difficult, were impossible. Beyond the window,
The sky would not let go of winter, and no one was warmed by the sun.
She closed her eyes and saw the two boys. The one in front
Looked straight ahead. His hat, jacket, and pants were so black
They could have been made of stone instead of cloth. His shoes
Had been repaired and repaired again. If he had any hopes left,
They were for a bowl of soup and a slice of gray bread that tasted
Of rye and lard. The other boy wore a jacket too small for him.
He was angry and, if she had asked, would have told her to throw
The pencil onto the floor and leave. There was something sadistic
In the way his eyes squinted at her. She could not force him
To recognize her or anyone. The boys carried an angel bent over
On a stretcher. A bandage covered the angel's eyes; there was blood
On one of her wings. The angel carried the exam answers in her hand,
A few white snowdrops she couldn't see. Her robe trailed along the ground.
The Polish poet knew it was too late. She'd grown old, and the exam
Was already over. But the boys refused to stop walking, and the angel
Still allowed herself to be carried, bent over on the stretcher. The Polish poet
Returned to her apartment, sat at her desk, and listened to the traffic outside.
She could hear footsteps in the hallway.

A Doppelgänger

> *Ere Babylon was dust*
> *The magus Zoroaster, my dead child,*
> *Met his own image walking in the garden.*
> —Percy Bysshe Shelley, *Prometheus Unbound*

Borges met his younger self on a park bench
In Geneva. Or, it might have been his older self;
These things are hard to figure out. I had
A doppelgänger also, but not me at a different age.
I discovered him when I gave a reading once
At a bar in Boston. Some people showed up
Expecting him and left when they realized
Their mistake. We never met, but I've seen
His picture. He had those long sideburns they
Call "mutton chops" that were popular back
In the 70s. Sometimes, friends mistake his books
For mine, at least one book of poetry and a work,
I believe, on Eastern religious practices. He
Traveled to India for sure, while I only know
Asia from museums. I suspect he was the more
Intelligent of the two of us. He could read Sanskrit
Like Eliot, but I don't know his poems. I avoided
Them on purpose, afraid I'd meet myself, with
Whatever consequence that might entail.
It's generally bad news to encounter your
Other self. Still, a few nights ago, I read online
That he'd died last year. I had to look away
From the screen. He wasn't that much older
Than I am. Now, the only chance we'll have
To meet will be on a park bench by Lake Geneva
Or walking in a garden in Babylon.

A Bench in Venice

He sits on a bench in Venice, staring at the Neva in December,
All his clothes purchased in Italy or the States, his coat wrapped
Around him the way a new language surrounds the old.

By the desk in the apartment, there are two typewriters, English
And Cyrillic, and a ream of white paper. Late for an appointment,
He hurries across the wooden bridge at the Accademia.

His heart beats fast; his body cries out for espresso and a forbidden
Cigarette. He wants to sit in the San Marco when the band is playing
And later eat cuttlefish cooked in its own ink, spooned

Over white polenta, white as a sail on the lagoon. But the truth is
He never sees white sails on the lagoon. Mostly, there have been
Water taxis and fishing boats, green ferries carrying

Automobiles destined for Trieste or the Balkans. Beside the statue
Of Garibaldi in the park, a couple shares a cup of strawberry gelato
In winter. He laughs reflexively. Garibaldi's statue lacks his trademark

Red shirt. He's wrapped in stone, the way the poet's wrapped in wool.
Water from the lagoon surrounds water flowing beneath the Bridge of Sighs.
All the water in the world mixes together. The Amazon flows

Through Florence, and the Nile through New Orleans. Rivers, like humans
Change their clothes, but water is always water. The Aegean,
The Black Sea, the Mediterranean, all taste of salt: each buys its

Underwear in Istanbul and Odessa, each wears the sky for a scarf.
The poet thinks of space folding around him, just as fungible as water
Or as all the sounds a human voice can make.

His chest still aches from surgeries.

The Hazelnut Child

A boy no bigger than a hazelnut, his parents
An aging couple who'd wished so hard
For a child that their wish, the same for both,
Created him . . . out of nothing but their wish.

The boy no bigger than a hazelnut, could
Make horses obey him by poking and pinching,
Whispering repeatedly, "Faster, faster!"
He ran errands, performed chores, triumphantly.

The boy no bigger than a hazelnut, nestled
In the feathers of a stork and flew to Africa
To make his fortune, as many did in those days.
He returned with a diamond — somehow.

A boy no bigger than a hazelnut, and his parents,
Wealthy from his adventure, moved to a great house —
Servants had to be careful where they stepped —
But he, Ulysses-like, grew bored and packed his bag.

A boy no bigger than a hazelnut,
His parents no longer alive,
Went off to sleep in a hazelnut grove,
And stayed there until he died.

Guilty Pleasures

When I'm alone, I stream films on Netflix or Amazon.
Often, they're fantasies, stories of young women and men who have
Magical powers, who struggle with monsters and dark forces. Some of them
Will sacrifice themselves to save their families or others they love. Some
Will be tempted, lost to incomprehensible evil. But the ones who
Interest me most are the devoted servants of darkness. Usually,
They've lived for centuries, perhaps demons, vampires, or some other
Species of villain. If they win, the sun will no longer shine brightly.
Night will encase us like the shell of a walnut or the way a wooden drawer closes
Tightly, not a sliver of light penetrating, nothing visible. The heroes
Are warned about this: the stakes are high. The darkness will destroy everything,
The alabaster towers, the peaceful villages, the cheerful taverns—
Nothing will be left. And this is what makes me wonder.
What reward do the evil ones expect? What comforts will they enjoy?
What pleasures, even sadistic pleasures, can they experience then?
Perhaps, they're like saints and expect nothing, doing what they do
Out of idealism, devoted to the destruction of Istanbul or New York,
London or Rome. Ascetics of nothingness, they may be without desire at all.
Perhaps they look at the world blindly and don't understand their battle
Was won long ago. The light that remained, the stuff of stories and films,
Was snuffed out by Alexander's phalanxes and Caesar's legions. Or perhaps,
We all drowned in the Red Sea and never knew it.

At the End of a Previous Century

From his small café table, a poet leans back
And recites a whole crown of sonnets
Without a mistake, his voice loud as church bells
On a winter Sunday, his eyes focused far off,
Staring at the future he and his audience expect
To begin any minute. All the clocks have stopped
Ticking, the streetlamps flicker, and inside the café,
With its wood-framed mirrors, tessellated floors,
And waiters with waxed mustaches,
The customers look up from their bottles
Of absinthe. The smell of anise, of alcohol,
Slips out onto the boulevard. Around the corner,
A cobblestone street runs downhill, perpendicular
To a river. There is no sound of traffic, and even
The smoke of blackened chimneys sinks
To the pavement. Everyone, everything, is
Listening except the housecat that rests
On the windowsill, who with a rough, pink tongue
Cleans his dusty fur and knows better than any
Of the others the irrelevance of words.

Jules Supervielle's Beret

His family was Basque, so the beret
Came naturally. The photograph's background
A bridge on the Seine, or the ocean outside
The harbor—the heart beats the same everywhere.
On the open sea, a sailor's longing
Gives birth to a child who can neither live
Nor die, an imagined French town where
No one lives. This takes place in the space
Of a heartbeat. At night, he rolls to his left
And feels the heart pump against his arm.
This is how life is measured. The drummer
Inside his chest keeps time and improvises.
He has long conversations with God, but
God is not forthcoming. Each morning,
The newspaper and coffee, hot rolls
And marmalade. Each morning
Unexpected. His heart has been bad
All his life. If he should dive into the waves,
They'd carry him back: Montevideo,
France, an unidentifiable suburb, sounds of
Passing cars and buses, a crane at the docks
Unloading cargo, algebra of wooden crates,
Blue ink and letters written in the clouds—
Not in French or Spanish, but a language
Spoken by birds who nest in the mountains.
Sometimes, they fly all the way to Paris.

One Sky Is Not Another

The sky in Barcelona
Is different from Miami's humid blue
Or the blue of Paris influenced
By paintings: some days pointillist,
Others impressionist. In New York, it's
Shaded by automobile exhaust and
Exhalations of people who live there.
In winter, you can see the steam from
Their mouths turning to small clouds,
And in summer, their sweat rises
Like prayers.

On Revenge

Cicero's head and hands were cut off, displayed
In the forum on Antony's orders. The hands
That wrote speeches against dictatorship, dried
In the sun, froze in Roman winter. The head
Was picked clean by birds, first eyes, later
The rest. An enemy's wife stuck hairpins
In his tongue. In time, Caesar Augustus regretted
Having allowed it. In time, Antony died too,
And none of it mattered.

Life at the Prado

When our politics in the United States
Becomes too depressing, I think how much
I'd like to live at the Prado, pass by
Each morning to say hello to Velásquez
And Goya, to make sure no new figures
Have crept into Bosch's Garden, to spend
Whole afternoons with Bruegel, then
Take a nap on the long couches and
Have coffee in the café before it closes.
The museum guards would all know me
And nod indulgently when I
Greet them in my bad Spanish. They
Might tell a new hire, "He's harmless,
He lives downstairs." I would have to
Be careful not to spend too much time
In one room or another—the paintings
Could come to expect my attention—
Caravaggio's frowns might deepen.
Clara Peeters might conceal her hidden
Self-portraits no matter how intensely
I stared. *Check for her reflection,
I'd tell myself, in the silver centerpiece.*
Then at night, I would stand by the exit
And wish everyone good evening as they
Went home to dinner, as they clutched
Their purchases from the gift shop, or
Passed by Ribera to retrieve their coats.

A Poem About the Mind

I wanted to write a poem about the mind,
But all I could think of were rain-slick sidewalks,

Traffic lights, and Chinese restaurants, the old-style
Cantonese-American kind, with bowls of stick-like
Fried noodles on every table. Then I wanted

To write a poem about cities, but I'd lived
In too many to pick out one or two. I remembered

Lightbulbs and the smell of auto exhaust in San José,
Of coffee and *tacos al pastor* in La Condesa,
Of cheese counters on the Upper West Side,

Smells of fish and gasoline on the Miami River
At night, water splashing against the dock. I wanted

To write a poem about the body. I thought it might
Be easier. But I didn't know what it was like to be
Alive in someone else's skin, to get up from the table

Somehow differently, walk with an unfamiliar
Movement of hips and legs. So, I started

With what I do know, how we move
Together in bed, pressing against each other,
Suddenly without names or faces, without arms,

Hands, buttocks—less conscious than the sheets
And mattress that bear our weight. I wanted,

I told you this, to write a poem about the mind,
But like that one-armed monk in the Zen
Story about Bodhidharma, when I looked

I couldn't find it.

Marsyas

What they never tell us about Marsyas
        is that he knew he would lose.
Apollo knew as well. The sky leaned down
        and whispered in the god's ear,
"No matter what he sings, you will beat him."
        The walls of Troy had risen at
Apollo's singing, but the human voice is
        small, no matter how poignant.
No element of nature helps Marsyas.
        He's tied to a tree, his skin
Ripped away in strips by the god's hand,
        his screams heard across oceans
And deserts, in the halls of government buildings
        and seaside resorts in winter,
In city streets when the office workers have
        gone home, in the alleyways behind
Restaurants, wedged between empty buckets
        of soy oil and lard, behind
The dumpster where something moves and
        then stops. Blood pools
At Marsyas's feet, soaking the brown earth,
        the tree roots, the grass red, sticky,
Drying black. Why challenge a god when he knew
        what would happen, how satyrs
And centaurs, hooves cracked open from running,
        would fall terrified into Poseidon's
Dark waves, how nymphs would hide behind
        Clothing racks in empty thrift shops
And below deck on fishing boats, how
        the smell of his death would sicken
Even hyenas and buzzards? The human voice
        is small compared to a god's voice.
Marsyas's flute is taken by Apollo, his skin
        draped over a tree limb.
Marsyas knew all this. Still….

Who's to Say

Who's to say these faces in the clouds aren't gods
Peering down from Olympian heights, beings
Sketched in vapor, vanishing into horses
And hillsides, vertical landscapes, emptiness
Of sky? Buddha and Moses feared images—
So did Plato—how real the shadows lamplit
On the walls of our cave. In the corners of
The living room, galaxies of dust turn in
Their slow waltz, almost invisible, weightless
As dreams. The dog twitches in his sleep, chasing
Something smaller than himself, something smelling
Of open fields in summer, of musk and shit.
He opens his eyes, confused, the way I am
When I'm trying to hold on to wherever
I was before my eyelids cracked to let in
Morning, chiaroscuro of curtains. The
Faces dissolve into time—not a process,
Just a way to measure what the world does and
We do. Last night, you had fever and asked me
To hold you as you slept, to keep you warm. Our
Bodies wrapped into each other, and you stopped
Trembling. I fell asleep on my side, my legs
Warmed by yours, finding comfort against your feet.
Nothing is ever how we remember it.

El Café del Sonámbulo

He wore a pinstriped suit and brown wool
Overcoat. He'd already finished
His coffee, but he still nibbled on
A roll. Crumbs fell to the tablecloth.
He opened a leather notebook with
Ivory-colored paper and wrote
A poem in green ink. I wanted
To ask all the questions I'd saved as
I read the *Residencias*, thought
How many varieties there are
Of loneliness, how they'd bloomed
From his chest, an English garden
Bordered by ribcage. I couldn't think
How to ask about the cost of it,
Shame, dysentery, an abandoned
Corpse in the street, night sweats and fever.
His fountain pen moved in neat circles,
But I couldn't see the script, the lines.
And, I don't know that he could see me
There, standing by the wooden table,
Plates and cups, the spoon balanced above
Some lumps of sugar. Was it me who
Spoke with him? Someone did. Words hung in
The air like brightly colored laundry
Almost dry, and Neruda, dead for
Fifty years, ordered one more coffee.

In Bogotá

The Gaitán museum in Santa Teresita had closed
During the pandemic and hadn't reopened. We
Drove past it, an aging white house in a green yard, but
The rest we had to imagine: the hat with a bullet hole,
The suit he was wearing, in a glass case, the one Vásquez
Describes in *La forma de las ruinas*. Your sister Pilar
Offered to drive, maneuvering her SUV through
Narrow streets and around cars blocking intersections.
On the way to Candelaria, a man was sitting outside
Wrapped in a poncho, drinking coffee. The sun
Slowly took the chill off the sidewalks and rooftops.
It was Saturday, and families walked between gray office
Buildings and movie theaters. Graffiti looped unintelligibly
On the walls. There was no parking anywhere we really
Wanted to go, so we kept driving. The Casa de Poesía Silva
Was closed too. I thought of books growing damp, sheets
Thrown over the furniture. We could have gone shopping
Or to a café, but instead, we drove back to our hotel in
Chapinero, the red-brick architecture of an English suburb,
Streets zigzagging up into the hills. Gaitán's murder had set off
A civil war that Americans didn't study when I was in school.
At least, North Americans didn't study it. The next day,
There was lunch at Pilar's, and we talked about the other civil war,
The one that caused you to leave Colombia for Miami. Later,
We both felt exhausted, drank coca tea for the altitude.

Reading Your Poem

Mi amor, I'm reading your poem, "The Unmade Bed,"
About a woman waiting for a man who's disappeared,
Probably taken away to be killed. Forty years ago
In your country, that happened to people you knew. You'd
Hear explosions when you were working at the university.
Later, like everyone else, you stopped by the supermarket,
Bought chicken and rice and went home to cook dinner.
Now you translate the narratives of women and men
Who are still leaving, as you left, after threats by
Mail or on the phone, a voice that says they've been
Tried and sentenced, that parts of them will be found
By the highway if they're lucky. The war is over now,
Mostly, but the threats are still there. Paramilitaries still
Demand taxes; the last guerillas rule villages far away
From the restaurants in Bogotá or Cali or the tourist
Ziplines near Medellin. At the National Museum,
We stood in front of Garay's painting of the Levite's
Concubine, raped and nude, mouth open, a corpse
Smeared with dirt—the man staring down at her
Seems surprised, his own guilt at having given her
To the mob completely forgotten. Garay was no fool.
He lived during civil war, and he knew what he was painting.
More than a century later, they're still finding bodies.
There're still unmade beds.

"So innocent are gods...."

> *So innocent are gods, they listen for praise like children.*
> —Rainer Maria Rilke, Stephen Mitchell tr.

So many prayers begin with *"Barukh ata Adonai...,"*
Imagining some unimaginable being listening
For our small, human-sized blessing, our gratitude for the bread
On the table, the cup of wine that holds only a few sips,
Gratitude disaster hasn't crushed our house to splinters,
Our bodies to their saggy, mechanical pumps, antique
Bellows shedding CO_2 and a few damp words.
We're grateful too for that dominion over the Earth,
The animals we roast on spits, all too aware
As we sit by the fire, it could so easily be us, our fat
Dripping down, hissing into the flames.
Created in that image, we touch our skin in disbelief—
So much softer than the hide of cattle or lions—
Is this membrane the image of something immortal? Do
Our eyes see through mountains, across deserts?
Instead, we fear the delivery truck that jumps the curb,
The angry politician who blames us for his unhappy
Childhood, the flood that drowns palaces, hotels, monuments,
The icy comet that this time doesn't pass us by.
So we bless, over and over again, releasing the holy
Hidden spark, healing the world that somehow never
Heals—all the time, knowing what could happen, hoping
The chemicals of our bodies stay just so, not too much salt or
Sugar, hoping that small blood clot won't float to the brain
Or heart, the influenza drifting through the air conditioning
Won't find its way to our noses and mouths, pale
Mimicry of something eternal, something listening,
Eager to hear our heartfelt blessings, our relentless praise.
Like Job, we refuse to curse God and die. We're
Smarter than that. Job got a new family, a new farm
And livestock, but we remember all the ones who
Didn't make it. The previous wife, sons, daughters,
Who used to sleep in the same beds and eat at the same
Table—and Job was OK with it, his loved ones
Fungible as air. All he had to do was praise.

IV. The Lives of Our Desire

What Gamblers Know

Gamblers are more honest than the rest of us.
They know we can only take what luck gives—
That when it's good, it's not because some virtue
Rests on our shoulders like a soldier's epaulets, and
That when it's not, there's no point to second-guess or
Blame ourselves, sit morose in cafés
Or on padded stools in diners, watching
In the steam swirling above the cup the shapes of
Lives we could have had and didn't. Gamblers know
Blaming doesn't help. It doesn't make the silver
Ball fall on red or black when the occasion warrants.
It doesn't make the card we need slide obligingly
Into our hands or a stack of chips grow like cornstalks
Out of dry soil. Sometimes, bad luck lasts
For years. Then, one day there's a perfect stillness.
The light reflects from puddles in the street,
But it doesn't blind us or make us wince. Then, a breeze
Just strong enough so we notice how it moves over
The Earth like dice on green felt, like a smile
On the face of a player who bet on zero or double zero
And somehow won, how it moves like luck itself,
A wave that picks us up and eventually lets us drop.
A gambler would know you didn't enter my life
Because of anything I said or did. A gambler
Would say it was luck, good luck, a perfect spin
Of the wheel, the card I would never have
Thought possible. He'd say, "Don't ask questions.
Don't imagine you did something to deserve this
Or worry that you didn't." He'd say it was luck,
That's all, and he'd be right.

How to Be a Tourist in Barcelona

On your second afternoon in town, do nothing.
Take a long bath. (There's a bathtub!) Dress in
Clothes that are relatively clean, go sit on the back

Terrace, and look up at the colors of the towels
And sheets hung on the neighbors' clotheslines.
Remember the boxes of wooden clothespins

Your great aunt used and the lines strung across
Her backyard. Here, blue and red shirts are hanging
From the railings of balconies along with fuchsia

Dish towels and gray sweaters. On another balcony,
There is an herb garden. You're too far away
To see what kind. That terracotta pot might be

Rosemary. To the east, the sun hits some corrugated
Roofing and casts a scalloped shadow down the side
Of an unpainted building. The bricks show through

In places. In the courtyard between buildings,
You will find nothing designed by Gaudi, only
The cries of gulls and pigeons, and a radio playing

A pop song you don't recognize. One building
Is being renovated, and men in long-sleeve t-shirts
And baseball caps are working on scaffolding.

In the courtyard, there are no monuments, but
It will make you remember Orwell, who thought
That for the briefest of moments Barcelona was

The best society humans had created. It will also
Make you think about what followed. That was
Only eighty-something years ago. These buildings

Stood here then. Their windows opened onto
The street battles between anarchists and communists,
Socialists, nationalists, and inevitably fascists.

The world did nothing to help. Orwell died
Of tuberculosis in England, but not before his
Prose eviscerated Auden for referring to "the

Necessary murder." Several pigeons—not a flock—
Move from one roof to another where there's
More sun. The sleeves of a black turtleneck flap

Lifelessly in the breeze. The sky is a pure,
Brilliant blue that denies history exists and that
Suffering matters. It doesn't even care about

Architecture and cathedrals. It only knows its
Own permanence. Stare up at it, and watch
The gulls and pigeons. There will be other afternoons

To be a tourist, to visit La Sagrada Familia,
The museums, and to take the cable car up Montjuïc.
For now, just sit on the terrace.

She Puts Down Her Book

She puts down her book and looks out
The window at snow filling the street and
Sidewalk, filaments of ice joining one twig
To the next, wind curling around the house
And the shed. Even though it's morning,
Night piles up in the corners. She is here
At the window, but her eyes see other places
As well, staring past wiper blades at highways
In the rain, her fingers touching the stratified
Wall of a canyon, her thumbnail rough
Against the ridges of a seashell. Each tree
Contains all trees: the live oak, the pear,
The coconut palm, the sequoia, the elm that
Turned yellow and died, the small lignum vitae
Once used to treat syphilis, make life preservers
For clipper ships, the seed of each, the root,
The bark, the leaf—each a catalog of all the rest,
Each stone is all stones, each sky all skies,
Each already present in memory and what's
Not yet memory, the square of a European city
Filled with cars and motorcycles, the exhaust
Of buses, a side street turned into a market,
Displays of apples and skinned rabbits
Hung by their hind feet from metal hooks,
Bright scarves sold at a booth, knit gloves and hats,
Brown mushrooms in boxes next to the potatoes.
Each sky is all skies. In this one, clouds like milky
Cataracts filter the sunlight. The cathedral barely
Casts a shadow, even though it's still morning,
And a gray-white glare barrels across
The terracotta roof tiles. She is here
At the window, but there also. Wrapped
In a wool coat, she sits on the cold iron
Of a café chair. The coffee is sweet.
The rolls taste of grain and butter.

It Never Rained

The whole time we were in Mexico City, it never rained. In the afternoon, at rush hour, the air above the streets was brown with dust. It felt hard to breathe. But at night, the sky was polished obsidian, and the moon ignored the light rising from the avenues. We walked over broken sidewalks and sudden curbs, making fun of our own stumbling. There were cafés lit with strings of yellow bulbs, and an improvised kitchen served tortillas and meat from a cart on the sidewalk. These days, I always think that whatever I'm doing I might be doing for the last time. I'll turn 70 in November, and I'm scared to add up all the things that could go wrong. Even without the desire for completion, so much seems incomplete. But maybe that's better. Who would want to die with all their socks and underwear washed? Ximena gave one of our tacos and some guacamole to the man selling candy.

Rabelais

Two editions of Rabelais reproach
Me from the bookshelf. This is the last year
Of my sixties. I haven't read either.
How much longer will God have patience with
Such a slacker? I've watched movies so bad
I could tell you the ending from the first
Shot, or at least the first bullets exchanged,
But I still have books with uncut pages—
And the languages I should have learned but
Didn't? What have I been doing with this
Time I've been awake? Baudelaire prayed for a
Poem that would justify him, allow
Him to feel he wasn't worse than all those
People he despised. I'm not confident
That any poem could justify me
For long. I've avoided hard work as far
Back as I can remember, and I can
Remember a long way back. Rabelais
May have been a good man, but his portrait
On the frontispiece looks mournfully at
My wandering attention. I've moved so
Many times, boxed his books and others, packed
Them in a moving van or the back seat
Of a car, picked them up without bending
My knees and paid a price for that—which makes
It even worse that they've gone unread. I've
Resisted buying Proust for much the same
Reason. Why make myself feel guiltier
Than I do already? If Baudelaire had
Known me, I'm pretty sure I'd have been one
Of those whom he despised. It's already
Dark outside, and I don't know what I did
Today besides fix lunch. *Mi amor*, I'll
Start brown rice steaming in the instant pot,
Get in the car, and drive downtown to bring
You here for dinner. We'll make each other
Laugh and invite Rabelais to share our
Roast chicken, green beans, a glass of our wine.
Nothing fancy, but I think he'd like it.

Without an Umbrella

I worry that I write too much about getting old.
Then think, no way—I write about lots of things:
A black and white duck pecking at the curb,
A sadness that keeps me company at dinner,
Rain on the roof, Cesária Évora singing,
General Tso's chicken from the take-out down the block,
And the gray-green paint on the walls of Browning's palazzo.
(It's hard to believe that anyone ever lived there.)
Granted, I remember people no longer here to
Remember me: Frank who played the trumpet
And liked red wine with Ximena's lentil soup,
Harold who'd bluffed Meyer Lansky at five-card stud,
My father who couldn't understand why he had cancer,
My mother who didn't understand that he had died—
Maybe my worries are right, partly right, or
A little wrong. Tonight, we tied our shoelaces
And walked beneath familiar, fast-moving clouds.
Ximena sat with me on a bench, the canal
Reflecting headlights as it always does,
Trees blacker than the water or the sky.
But this time a hard Miami rain chased us
Home, wet clothes stuck like Band-Aids to our backs,
Our socks sponging the water as we ran
To the front door of the house, shivering, alive.

Conjugations

Mi amor, outside I can hear rain
Dripping from the gutters on the roof
In the morning, there'll be a puddle
On the asphalt, and ducks will
Leave *mierda* by the walkway.
But now, there're just trees
Blocking the neighbors' lights,
Clouds fumbling their way
Across the night sky. It's hard
To see the clock without my glasses,
But I'm sure it's late. My lips
Brush hesitantly against
Your spine, your neck.
I don't know much Spanish, but
I whisper a few words, simple ones:
Te quiero, te deseo, te toco, te beso.

Watching a Hurricane Pass to the West

Light through the window fades to a dull-
Blue wash of water, rain on the roof,
A Bakelite radio stuck between
Stations, the aloe vera plant on
The patio a deepening green.
There's a brief lull between bands; then it
Resumes, shadows grown darker, as the
Sun, invisible, sinks on the storm's
Other side, the Gulf of Mexico.
Meanwhile, coffee in hand, I'm standing
Here listening to rain as modern
Jazz, shades of blue light ricocheting
Off the wooden fence, tree limbs in their
Odd stooped-over dance. It's probably
Nothing anyone should make sense of,
Much less enjoy. Again, there's a leak
In the roof over my son's bathroom.
Water bubbles beneath the paint. I
Think of the cost and take a breath. The
Storm drips slowly from the light fixture.

Balconies

Beyond our lives are other lives, ones
We might have lived but didn't. Cities
We visited asleep, read about
In guidebooks or glossy magazines,
Photographs of olive trees older
Than Chartres, cafés where waiters know
Already we'll be there for hours,
Our cups empty, staring through the glass
At passersby under umbrellas,
Running from the cold November rain.
Beyond our lives are cobblestone streets
Flowing up hillsides, rivers in reverse.
At the top, stone fortifications
Constructed by Caesar, by the Huns,
Visigoths, Moors, or Napoleon.
Below, landscapes famous for battles
Or poets—Machado might have stood
Here and watched the sun sink to the west.
Beyond our lives are the lives we've lived
(Forgotten?), magnolia blossoms
Outside my bedroom window, the street
I'd stare at late at night, cars going
Somewhere, the Chinese restaurant on
Milam Street that stayed open till dawn,
Or later, apartments in New York
And Boston, metallic smell of steam
From the radiator in winter,
The remainder tables in bookstores—
To blame for my odd education—
And your life by the Rio Cali,
The steep green hillsides, salsa playing
On a radio, crazy traffic
In the evenings, civil war, and threats
On the telephone. Beyond these lives
Are the lives of our desire, Madrid,
Velázquez at the Prado, Goya,
Pulpo a la gallega, bread warm
From the oven, wines we've never tried,

Neighborhoods we've never made our own,
Balconies where we look out on all
The lives we haven't yet imagined.

"The Other Day"

You say *el otro día,* and it could be any time,
An afternoon of sunlight on red bougainvillea
Or a time when the canals were dark

As mahogany and filled with rain.
Two days ago or a hundred—we've held
Each other for a long time now. I've memorized

The bedspread at your apartment, the weave
Of the cloth, the colors grown muted.
You want to replace it, but I argue no—

You just got it the other day.

Andalusia

At the train station in Córdoba, we rented an aging
Gray Renault and drove to the mountains, the car's
Maintenance light flashing red the whole time.
From both sides of the road, rows of olive trees
Extended their camouflaged limbs, saluting
The afternoon sun, while small rivers carried
Dust and run-off to the south.
On the hill above Almodóvar del Río, the towers
Of a castle, mirage-like, stood without blinking.
The highway pointed north, and the engine strained
Until I shifted to a lower gear. Then—again,
On both sides of the road—there were orange groves,
White flowers and early fruit, the scent
Of oranges all around us and inside
Our rented car.

In Puebla de los Infantes, lunch was almost over
When we found a parking space on a street
Cut into the side of a hill, a row of cars perched
At 45 degrees, brakes firmly engaged.
One restaurant was still open. We ate
Quickly—Ximena's reading was in less than
An hour. ¿Dónde está la biblioteca, por favor?
"Drive down the hill and ask someone else," two
Andalusian ladies replied. By chance, we saw
The sign, and a man exercising a brown
Stallion by the parking lot. Ximena read well,
Poems about her country, her parents, our life
In Miami. The crowd was happy to hear her.
She'd come all the way from Colombia, where
There are also mountains, but instead of olive
Trees and oranges, there are mangoes and bananas,
Guerrillas and paramilitaries.
Another poet gave her a copy of his book, and
We drove back to Córdoba in the dark.
I stopped at a gas station to buy bananas
And oranges.

A Question

In the Gothic Quarter, our friend pointed
Out indentations cut like a tally in the old
Roman wall. There had been a market
Here, and the butchers had sharpened
Their knives against the gray stone—
Centuries of sharpening, the way canyons
Are shaped by water, the way we're shaped
By deaths, marriages, divorces, by the books
We've read and remembered, by the ones
We wish we remembered. *Mi amor*, are we
The stone shaped by so many knives, or
Are we the knives sharpened by stone?

How Far Away the World Seems

It's midnight, and we're back in Miami,
Still a little jetlagged, still thinking
About Spain, the fields of small olive trees,
The persistent scent of orange blossoms,
The white-barked plane trees along the avenues
In Barcelona, a city held by two mountains
And the Mediterranean. In Madrid about now,
Sleepers roll onto their sides, shifting
Their bodies in the last hours of dreaming,
Before coffee, before the metro or the office.
Perhaps, they sleep with the windows open,
The sound of birds waking, of early traffic
Rising into their dreams, a figure who
Urges them to hurry, the statue of Goya
Outside the Prado calling to them:
"Whatever you're looking for in your sleep,
Find it now." Above their heads, small
Monsters circle, just the way they do here
When reason's too tired to hold them at bay.
Goya imagined St. Anthony, the poor and
Sick circling him to be healed, angels struggling
With enormous folds of fabric, uncertain
Of their task. Whose robes were those?
In Miami, the restaurants at the shopping
Mall closed hours ago; the parking lot's
Empty except for the Salvation Army trailer
Where people leave their old televisions,
Clothes, and children's toys. The night
Watchman drives his white pickup around
The corner, its yellow lights visible
All the way to the canal.

Drinking Chai on a Mild Afternoon in January

Florida sunlight moves through the leaves
Like x-rays but in color, a dappled green shining
Across the fence, and above the asphalt tiles
Of the neighbor's new roof, a huge old oak is
Etched in gold. The last few years, we haven't had
A lot of days like this one. I called you today
To tell you the sky was almost as blue
As it was in Barcelona last April. I remember
Watching sea gulls circle the apartment buildings
And then fly back to the beach and the port.
A few days ago, I happened to see my photograph
Of that white pigeon in Córdoba. It was perched
On an air conditioner above the tables where
We were sitting outside, eating our fried calamari
And drinking wine at lunch. *Mi amor*, what becomes
Of memories like these when we're no longer here
To bring them to mind, to call up a narrow street
Filled with tables, waiters darting from one to the other,
Taking orders, delivering bocadillos, cervezas, espressos?
There was sunlight there also, when the sun was directly
Overhead or still not sunk below the roofs and balconies.
Other people will remember avenues in Barcelona,
The plane trees with their white bark and their leaves
That remind me of maples. These experiences belong
Only to us. Other people will have their own moments,
But not quite the same as ours, framed by the years
Before we met, by our disappointments and our—
What to call it—surprise at each other's existence:
Nights when we talked about Borges on the phone,
About how you came to Miami, about how I came
Here as well. Earlier, I saw buzzards coasting
High up, on the currents, anti-poetically looking
For something dead that they could eat. They're not
Like the crows who're interested in hamburger buns
And leftover pizza. Once, we were walking down
A street near the park and saw a group of them gathered
Around some unidentifiable roadkill. You were as
Excited as if they'd been giraffes, and told me all

About their digestive systems. After us, no one
Will remember that mundane, brutal, and somehow
Comic scene, but maybe it's best. This way, it
Belongs to us, like the sky in Barcelona, or that
Narrow street in Córdoba. Only in words can we
Pass them on to someone else. I'm looking outside,
Where it's starting to get dark early, the way it does
In winter here—night as surprising and sudden as
What I felt when we met—the moon rising just
As it already has in Spain and as it will soon above
The cathedral and the library we saw in Puebla
And above the mountains in Cali.

Asleep

We turn toward each other, breath
Steady, eyes moving beneath their lids.
We might as well be statues for all
We know then. In my dream, I ask my
Father what he thinks of a poem. (He's
Non-committal.) In yours, perhaps your
Mother shows you a recording of
A Beethoven sonata and asks you to play it
On the stereo. My father is wearing
A tweed jacket and is younger than
I remember. Early morning light cuts
Through the shutters—my eyelids
Flicker, an old film projector at the end
Of a reel. I'm planting a mango tree
In shallow topsoil, using the shovel to
Break the layer of brittle, white stone
A few inches beneath the surface. I'm
Trying to make space for the roots. I don't
Know what you've been dreaming and can't
Remember the stories I've dreamed either.
All I know is that I've moved closer to you,
Can feel your breath on my cheek.

What We Know, What We Can't Know

Late at night, we were out walking. It's
A time when the only shapes that cross
The darkness are cats or opossums,
Their eyes reflecting passing headlights.
But this didn't move anything like
An opossum or a cat. It was
Darkness outlined on darkness until
It lifted its wings and floated ten
Or twenty feet straight ahead. I said
To Ximena, "It's some kind of bird."
But I couldn't see more. Then, it flew
Again, wings enormous, only the
Shadow of an outline, and silent—
Just a glimpse in profile before it
Rose between the rooftops and was gone.
"It's a crane," I repeated, first to
Myself and then to Ximena. "It's
A crane at night, maybe lost, maybe
Looking for its mate, awake somewhere,
Another shape in the dark, waiting."

At the Museo Nacional

> *Por las velas, el pan y el chocolate*
> *Yo combato, tú combates, él combate*
> —José Manuel Marroquín*

When we found Garay's painting, it was
In a glass display, not quite obscured
By antique implements to brew hot
Chocolate. The young round-faced servant
Was dressed to go shopping. She had a
Black shawl across her shoulders. Her skirt
Was clean and embroidered, and she might
Have passed for a lady, except for
Her bare foot stepping into the street.
Behind her, a gentleman in black
With a top hat turned to examine
Her figure, while a woman (his wife?)
Also dressed in black, half-hidden in
Shadow, politely looked at the door.
This, that poem tells us, is what we
All fight for: the candles, the bread, and
Chocolate. The land had already
Been distributed to wealthy men,
Who would make *best use* of it and pay
Garay to paint their portraits holding
Black canes with silver handles. Outside,
We were introduced to a poet
And a well-known actress—not known to
Us—and we squeezed into a van with
Your sisters and the poet to find
A good place to get broth or coffee.
La Candalaria was bulging
With tourists and vendors selling them
Souvenirs and arepas. A man
Dressed in a wool poncho circled the
Block, holding the reins of a llama.
It was getting cold. You shivered and
Wrapped your new shawl across your shoulders.
At one end of the street, Plaza de

Bolívar. At the other, mountains,
Green above powerlines and low clouds.

* Ironically or not, the painting by Epifanio Julián Garay Caicedo, *Por las velas, el pan y el chocolate*, (Ca. 1870) takes its title from these lines. Their author, Marroquín, later went into politics, as a conservative, and twice became president of Colombia.

Miami, End of Winter

It's early February, but I can already feel
Sunlight making the air uncomfortable,
Too warm. The mango trees have been blooming
For a couple of weeks now. When they bloom early
And there's a cold snap, the fruit doesn't set.
This year, there could be no mangos in summer.
I stare for a minute at the black surface of the canal,
Water draining slowly to Biscayne Bay, where
Mangroves and mosquitoes cluster along the muddy shore.
The canal is pretty much like always, quiet,
Hiding fish, alligators the signs tell me not to feed.
Is anybody really dumb enough to feed them—and if
They were, what would they feed them, the family pet?
I keep walking. Alongside the path, the county has
Planted dogwood and some so-far unidentified shrubs.
One by one, they're being dried by the sun and then
Knocked down by storms—a bad idea to begin with,
And one that hasn't gotten better with age. Between
The power lines and the asphalt path, there's
Only grass and the wind that blows between
The shopping mall and the electrical station.
At night, you can see constellations and the lights
Of planes flying toward the Caribbean or
East toward Europe, but in the middle
Of the afternoon, there's just a blue, dry
Emptiness that the sky holds, then releases.
I stand here and watch it fall.

Such Hunger

In my sleep, I hear you shout, "*¡Qué hambre!*"
But I don't know what hunger you see or feel or that
I only imagine you see or feel. In *Galería Alameda,*
There was a table piled high with *moras*, blackberries,
And large flies covered them, just as black, almost
Indistinguishable, a table wet with juice, with
Moscas and berries. From metal beams hanging above
The narrow aisles, there were haunches of cattle,
White fat and dark red flesh. What hunger did you mean?
We ate fresh mangos and granadillas. Outside, there
Were carts, strings of orange *chontaduro*, the busy
Streets. Or was it *my* hunger, something so large I was
Swallowed by it, carried like Jonah across an ocean?
I'm walking with you somewhere else, maybe Bogotá
At night, streets that climb up into the hills or loop
Around so it's easy to get lost. There's a tall man
With a dog, asking for money. We're trying to get to
A place we know, maybe the bright windows of a hotel
Or where your sister will pick us up in her car.
In the half-light of a restaurant, we eat octopus
And grilled fish. We're both hungry. I stroke your arm
While we wait for the next course, the food overpriced,
Too elegant to make us full. Afterwards, we return
To your apartment for coffee, and I remember six years ago,
When you first invited me for dinner, how much
I wanted you, how hungry I was.

Happiness in the Tropics

It's supposed to be ignorant, a moment
When fingers touch your wrist lightly, or

When you notice that the leaves and roots
Of the orchid are green and just as alive
As the blooms dangling up above them.

The tomatoes in the bowl turn more deeply
Red each day. *They should be eaten tonight.*

Someone will say this happiness is trivial,
That nearby, people no different from us
Are hungry, grieving, or in pain. They're

Right, but I think of those wild rose bushes
I saw growing in Key West. No one knows

How they arrived or survived, tropical, profuse,
A tangle of vines, thorns, and raining petals.
They shouldn't be there, but they are.

Unlike Romeo and Juliet

We've never had to part at morning. The light
Crossing from window to far wall has always
Been an annoyance or reminder to make
Coffee, a reminder I ignore. Instead,
I untangle the sheets and roll your way, my
Arm the vanguard for the rest of me. You sleep
On your right, resisting waking up, and I
Surrender to your lethargy, familiar
Scent of your hair, your cheek flushed from the pillow.
I press my head against your back, shamelessly.

At Your Apartment

Looking out the window in your living room,
I can see a late-night traffic jam in Wynwood,
A line of red lights going nowhere—
In the distance, office buildings, a mural
Illuminated and silent. We've stayed here on
Weekends for seven years now. Everything
Has changed, and nothing has changed.
The neighborhood is more upscale than it was.
Sometimes, there will still be panhandlers in
The parking lot at the supermarket, but the new
Buildings going up are luxury condos with
Doormen out front, yoga classes in the gym.
The Brazilian restaurant with appetizers and good
Wine closed during the pandemic. When it
Reopened it was a Peruvian fast-food joint where
Everything came out of the freezer. We ate there
Once and never went back. Now, we make our own
Bread and eat sandwiches on Saturdays. Tomatoes
Ripen on the dining-room table. For seven years,
We've held each other at night, sometimes lightly,
Sometimes so close it feels like we're trying to push
Inside each other's skin, pillows, blankets falling
To the floor. *Me encanta estar en cama contigo.*
It doesn't matter how many times I've said it
Or how many nights we've spent like this. We
Both know how fragile it all is, how deep inside,
A cell could be dividing recklessly or a small
Clot of blood could be moving to the brain.
Love won't protect us from that—or anything else.
I peel a naval orange and ask if you'd like half.
They're good this time of year.

Ximena Refuses

Ximena refuses to accept that we are old.
She says people live longer now, and we are still young.
After all, we still work, still follow politics, still cook and make love.
If we walk a little slower or treat our backs and knees with more consideration,
What difference does it make? She watches the ducks who spend long afternoons
In the parking lot outside my door. Water from the air conditioning
Drips down the rain spout. They wade in it and drink what they can.
How do you tell the age of a duck? None of them seem geriatric.
Last year, there were ducklings who followed them and stumbled
Toward the golf course or the street. Sometimes, I see a bundle
Of broken feathers by the curb, but that one may have been careless, not old.
It was different with my dog. I could see that he had aged, grown thinner,
Lost his teeth and appetite. I don't want to be old the way he was.
I'd rather nod my head and agree with Ximena. People live longer now.
We're still young.

Sobremesa

The dinner finished, the wine bottle
Still not empty, termite nymphs circling
The overhead lamps, the glass door
To the patio opaque, reflecting
Faint images of ourselves, a few
Moths, one of those Dutch interiors
But without a ray of light entering
Through a window—
We are shadows of our own
Reflections. We stare at our empty
Plates, at leftovers on the table,
But only because we need some place
To rest our eyes. The vases
Above the cabinet wait for us
To resume conversation, stories
About politics or the private affections
Of not-so-famous authors. We
Disappoint them. Safe from dust,
The fluted Bohemian
Goblets tremble a little next
To the porcelain, and the rose-glass
Fingerbowls stand awkwardly on each
Other's shoulders. My mother would
Only put them out for holidays, and
Now, they may resent as parvenues
The vodka glasses I purchased in Italy.
Regardless, none of them have been
Used in years. Why do I keep them still,
Like the books from my grandfather's
Library, pages barely held together,
Unreadable but still wedged, sentries,
On the highest shelf? If they have
A place in my life, I don't know
What it is. There's a portrait of
My grandmother and my mother,
Who'd insisted her doll be painted
As well. The painter, Louis Betts,
Tossed her in, stiff-armed, with

A minimum of strokes. It makes me
Smile to imagine his pique. He'd
Come all the way from Chicago.
This was before the Depression,
Before the house was sold, and
The chauffeur let go. Now, it
Doesn't matter. My mother's
Been dead for almost thirty years,
And whatever she hoped for me
Doesn't matter either. I tell you
How, if I were younger, I might
Start all over, in another country,
Maybe even another language.
Why have I carried with me all
These books and paintings, the china
I've never used, the linen tablecloths
Taking up room in the closet, too
Big to fit my table? There's a
Daguerreotype of my great-grandfather,
Printed on copper. I only know
A few stories about him—he wanted
His children to be educated, he owned
A store, he refused to allow German
To be spoken in his house and had
Left Alsace to avoid the Prussian army.
Maybe there's a genetic desire to be
Somewhere else or someone else. Maybe
There's also an antithetical desire
To hold on to curios, books, gilt-edged
Cups, to find a home in objects and
Memories. You tell me about a silver
Tray with your parents' initials—you
Brought it with you in a suitcase
From Colombia. I think about your
Apartment in Miami, how you made it
So separate from the world outside.
We are already somewhere else, already
Someone else. The home we make
For each other has nothing to do
With objects and memories, with cities

On a map, or streets lined with mailboxes
And driveways, or the walks we've taken
Late at night by the canal, or the mall's
Empty parking lot. The home we make
Is here at this table, in the stories we've
Told and probably repeated, in the way
Our hands touch involuntarily as we talk,
How we look at each other as we carry
The leftovers to the refrigerator and
Our dishes out to the sink.

About the Author

George Franklin practices law in Miami. *A Man Made of Stories* is his fourth full-length collection with Sheila-Na-Gig Editions, complementing *Remote Cities* (2023) *Noise of the World* (2020) and *Traveling for No Good Reason* (winner of the Sheila-Na-Gig Editions manuscript competition in 2018). His chapbook, *What the Angel Saw, What the Saint Refused* (2024) and *Poetry & Pigeons: Short Essays on Writing* (2025) are also from Sheila-Na-Gig. Franklin authored as well the dual-language collection, *Among the Ruins / Entre las ruinas* (translated by Ximena Gómez and published by Katakana Editores, 2020), and a chapbook, *Travels of the Angel of Sorrow* (Blue Cedar Press, 2020). He is the co-translator, along with the author, of Ximena Gómez's *Último día / Last Day* and co-author with Gómez of *Conversaciones sobre agua / Conversations About Water* (Katakana Editores 2019 & 2023).